THE INNER PATH TO

ALPHA

Arlen J.

Godset Publishing
www.arlenj.com

ISBN: 979-8-9909850-0-1 (paperback)
ISBN: 979-8-9909850-1-8 (ebook)

Ordering Information:
Special discounts are available on quantity purchases by corporations, associations, and others. For details, visit www.arlenj.com.

TABLE OF CONTENTS

INTRODUCTION

If you're going to be excellent or elite, you've got to do special things. You have to have special intensity. You have to have special focus. You have to have a special commitment and drive and passion to do things at a high level and a high standard all the time.

— Nick Saban

Every morning, I wake up feeling tanked—not what you'd expect from an experienced mindset coach. Even if everything is going well for me, I wake up with very little excitement about my day. I've been this way since I was a child. Even the effort of getting out of bed and getting started seemed like too much effort. To help, my mother started me on coffee around my second attempt at second grade. She called me "blue boy" back then. When I was older, I asked her why she called me that. "You always looked so sad," she said.

As a teenager, sluggish mornings coupled with poor self-talk often sent me into a tailspin. Unconscious and unchecked, my bad mornings became bad days, weeks, months, and so on. "Who's that angry-looking young man at the back of my church?" A priest once asked that question to my mother, knowing exactly who I was. It was his way of making his point. I was angry at the world, and it showed.

For many years I was addicted to my anger, and I was unconscious of it. Anyone who has been there knows what a trap anger can feel like. It stems from being able to recognize your own talents and abilities but not being able to get out of your own way long enough to do anything about them. I was in an endless cycle of self-sabotage, or so it seemed.

It wasn't until I began looking inward at myself, my mindset, and my personal conscious command that I started to turn things around.

My path to conscious command was long and paved with many relatable stories about adversity and triumph. I could share how I grew up in a hostile environment despite its outward appearance, or how I lived in my car for five years while building a business from the ground up.

I could tell you how a childhood trauma reawakened inside me while attempting to summit Mt. Shasta in the summer of 2018 and how the whole thing still haunts me to this day. But I want to give you much more than just an inspiring story of pulling myself back from the brink.

Many experts agree that inspiration and motivation are fleeting, while discipline is king. Yet, I feel very few experts offer any real definition or mechanics for achieving said discipline.

Boxing champion Mike Tyson has described discipline as "doing what you hate to do like you love it."[1] Although sometimes true, it takes a special kind of focus to command those moments in any real-time way. To get the mindset to consistently show up to do the things that one hates to do or isn't used to doing for any extended period of time takes a special kind of "intensity, focus, commitment, drive, and passion." It will take a special type of mindset—a reflexive mindset.

I want to give you the gritty truth about achieving that mindset and the concrete tools that ultimately set me, and many others like me, free. *The Inner Path to Alpha* is a look into the power of the Internal Monologue System (IMS) and the alpha brain wave-length synergy, how you can use it for your own success and to stop self-sabotaging.

Please keep in mind that the advances we seek in life aren't always the result of learning something new but from being reminded of the things we already know. May this book help reveal what you already know and remind you of who you already are. You're a bad motherfucker!

---

1 Mike Tyson (@Mike Tyson), "Discipline is doing what you hate to do like you love it," X (Twitter), March 25, 2022, 10:38 a.m., https://twitter.com/MikeTyson/status/1507396440888209412.

CHAPTER 1

WHAT MAKES A MAN OR WOMAN ALPHA?

The traditional alpha image was forced into the 21st century and presented under false pretenses, similar to the Trojan horse. That ancient form of subterfuge led to the historical defeat of the men of Troy, similar to how millions of men in the quest to become alpha feel defeated today. The ubiquity of social media and other digital communications has led today's men and women down a path of reflexive hesitance and subconscious incongruity. But the true and often overlooked scientific definition of "alpha" is hiding in plain sight. Moreover, getting men and women back on the path to enlightenment is essential.

ALPHA WOLF STUDIES

What is generally accepted as an alpha today is derived from research that studied wolves in captivity, not in their natural environment. The original researchers are now changing their stances after learning that captive animals are essentially synonymous with incarcerated humans and their behaviors. Dr. David Mech, founder of the International Wolf Center and author of the book *The Wolf: Ecology and Behavior of an Endangered Species*, has been studying wolf behavior for more than 60 years.[2] In his book, published in 1981, he wrote that wolves win control of the pack by fighting other male wolves. That behavior is exactly what is observed with incarcerated men getting in violent confrontations over territory in prisons.[3]

Dr. Mech then published the paper "Alpha Status, Dominance, and Division of Labor in Wolf Packs" in 1999. In it, he reversed his original position of nearly two decades earlier after he observed wolves in the wild. Incredibly, Dr. Mech observed no or little fighting for dominance in the wild like he had observed with wolves in captivity.

Despite ordering his publisher to stop printing the 1981 book due to his new evidence and subsequent mootness of said book, the publisher continues printing and selling his book. Mech has made clear that the term "alpha male," as it is currently accepted, is false and based on faulty research. Nevertheless, both the violence and fighting of captive wolves, which have come to define alpha males, remains with near unanimous scientific consensus today, with little effort being made for public awareness of Mech's 1999 update.[4]

---

2   "Home," Dave Mech, accessed March 7, 2024, https://davemech.org/.

3   L. David Mech, *The Wolf: Ecology and Behavior of an Endangered Species* (Minneapolis, Minnesota: University Minnesota Press: 1981).

4   L. David Mech, "Alpha Status, Dominance, and Division of Labor in Wolf Packs," *Canadian Journal of Zoology* 77 (1999): 1196–1203.

I too grew up with that inaccurate image. I grew up with six older brothers—my own personal wolf pack—who were at least 12 years my senior and were tough as shit. I got whooped on a lot from a generation that whooped on people. The idea of being an alpha or being a man came to me in the form of toughness and how much you can take.

Unfortunately, my parents were not a model of real leadership. By the time I was born, my parents were tired from raising kids. My dad was in his 50s and my mom was 41. They'd already raised six kids each from previous marriages. When they got together it was like the TV show *The Brady Bunch* but double the kids on both sides. So, I was a bit of the "out of sight, out of mind" child. My siblings spoke Spanish like my parents did, but I wasn't brought up to speak it with them. Instead, it was something my parents used to exclude me from the conversation. I was on a separate island, and I felt it. I constantly felt separated from the pack. It didn't bode well for me in the face of adversity, which came to me as my brothers at that time of my life. Even though I was tough and sometimes ready to stand up for myself, I was too volatile for that crap.

I was constantly in distress in terms of what leadership and alpha meant to me, though I didn't think of it in those terms at the time. Since my parents were older, the model they presented was "old school." I was raised to believe that the man was the "income, the problem-solver, the provider, and the leader." Women stayed at home. While that relationship may work for some family dynamics, it should be a personal choice, not a requirement. Like Dr. Mech's original finding, that idea was an outdated belief in what it meant to be alpha, but it was years before I understood that.

EFFECTS ON YOUNG MEN IN THE DIGITAL AGE

The correlation between alpha wolves and alpha men became mainstream ideology soon after Mech's book was published in 1981. But it really took off in the late 1990s. A handful of years later in 2005, Neil Strauss published *The Game: Penetrating the Secret Society of Pickup Artists*, which chronicles his experience in the "seduction community" online, where he and other men learn to become pickup artists who seduce women.

Though Strauss's book received fairly good reviews (3.74 stars out of 5 on Goodreads), the critical responses had a consistent tone—misogyny, lack of self-confidence and self-awareness. Several reviewers pointed out how most of the men stayed in the confines of their online communities, their comfort zones, versus venturing out and actually trying to communicate with women.[5]

Both Mech's original publication and Strauss's book promote an inaccurate idea of the alpha male and set a new benchmark for men. Both convey the idea that "being alpha" refers to men who could have what they wanted, when they wanted it. Men bought right into it. The only plausible condition in which this definition of alpha male holds true is, again, if they are taken out of their natural environments and placed into confined spaces such as prison and online forums.

Young Millennials and Generation Z men gravitated to spaces like 4chan and 8chan to create similar environments as described

---

5   Neil Strauss, *The Game: Penetrating the Secret Society of Pickup Artists* (New York: HarperCollins, 2005).

in Strauss's book. The term "incel" is short for "involuntarily celibate," and is a common insult to some and a compliment to others. These young men complained that women hate them, which makes them involuntarily celibate, and that there is nothing they can do to change it. But they feel like alpha males in their confined spaces, their web spaces, and thus do not attempt to communicate with women in real life.

Sadly, men (and women) are bombarded right now with influences through social media and pop culture that circle around what it means to be alpha. We're oversaturated with influences. There have been recent movements to curb the old-school meaning of alpha, but they've taken societal influences in the opposite direction, adding to the confusion of what alpha means or should mean.

Some people are still trying to promote the old alpha way, like Andrew Tate, who became the most Googled man in the world for a time, because of it. He has the old pop-culture idea of the alpha male being aggressive, loud, and taking what he wants when he wants. A lot of people are gravitating toward his demeanor because he's standing up, being vocal, and because he is intelligent and articulate.[6]

Even after his arrest and being accused of rape and child trafficking, people have been all over him and drawn to his messaging. While he might have some intelligent things to say, what gets him

---

6   "Who Is Andrew Tate? One of the Most Googled Person in the World," *The Economist Times,* October 24, 2022, https://economictimes.indiatimes.com/news/international/us/who-is-andrew-tate-one-of-the-most-googled-person-in-the-world/articleshow/94421929.cms.

in trouble is that he's too cocksure–presumptuously and arrogantly confident.

So, why have people flocked toward him?

It's because in this digital age, pop culture is going in the opposite and misguided direction with representations of alpha, and Andrew Tate epitomizes that old-school alpha mindset. To be clear, his audience is holding onto that old thought process, regardless of how outdated it is.

I've watched his videos, and although he's smart, he speaks with such anger and venom. Angst begets angst, and I don't gravitate to someone like that because I can feel the anger in his words. Anger isn't the right way to effect change. Not if you believe in frequency.

Frequency is the law of attraction. You have to think of yourself as energy that's attracting like energy. If you're always angry, then you'll attract angry energy.

Even though I'm not seeing the traditional, pop-culture alpha-male representations as often anymore, the lack of positive alpha influences is just as damaging as incorrect alpha influences. It also opens the door for people like Andrew Tate to continue to misrepresent alpha.

Sadly, pop culture and the digital age have left men and women, both young and old, lost and confused as to their roles in society. Their muddled thinking is clearly proven by a large number of men—40,500 a month to be exact—who are searching for the term "alpha male" on Google.[7] In their quest to be alphas, they have also been conditioned to believe a fallacious definition of what makes a man alpha. The only alpha men or women to exist, by any scientific standards, are those who operate from the alpha brain wavelength.

MY JOURNEY

My own journey to alpha began with confidence. It was the "end all, be all" for me. I didn't feel like I had it, and I kept asking myself, "How do I get there?" In my acting career, I had all the tools I needed to be confident, but inside, I wasn't feeling like an alpha.

All through high school, college, and until my 30s, I dabbled in stage acting. It was more of a hobby for me, something I did for fun that was fulfilling. Then I got my big break in television.

When I started TV acting, I had this look. I could be a soap opera star, I could be the bad guy in a movie… in fact, I played both types on the daytime drama, *The Young and the Restless*. I could do this or that, I could do anything. But it wasn't my look that helped with my confidence. It was my understanding of the power of words and how they could affect people.

And then something strange happened. As quickly as it came, I lost my purpose with acting.

---

7   "Which Socio-Hierarchy Personality Types Are the Most Favored Google Search in the First Half of 2023?" The Pleasant Personality, January 29, 2024, https://thepleasantpersonality.com/most-favored-socio-sexual-personality-types-in-google-search-in-the-first-half-of-2023/.

We may spend our whole life climbing the ladder of success, only to find when we get to the top that our ladder is leaning against the wrong wall.
— **Thomas Merton via Allen Raine**

When I first began acting it was from a desire to prove shit to people. I had spent years as a vagabond moving from city to city with nothing to show for it. I knew I could be "seen" as an actor on TV, which would show that I had moved past my self-sabotaging ways and had become successful. Things started happening for me quickly as an actor, but I wasn't trying to be an actor for myself.

As soon as I realized that I lost my purpose with acting, I deflated and lost my drive. It felt like my life was spiraling out of control. But from the ashes, I found a new purpose. Since I was already aware of the power of words, I began to talk passionately to myself and others about mindset and conscious awareness and to focus on frequency—the law of attraction.

The group I was part of at the time, my acting community, looked at me like I was nuts. They'd say things like, "Go back to acting. You're great at it." They loved me for the performances, but that wasn't the "me" I wanted or needed to be. It surely wasn't going to save me from my self-sabotaging ways.

Walking away from acting was a heavy decision. I was represented by the best Soap Star manager in the business. I had a film, TV, and commercial agent/manager to boot. Representation like that can be elusive for a lot of artists, but for me, it came quickly. At the time, that kind of representation felt like a guarantee for success.

Within months of arriving in L.A., I was recurring as "Isaac" on *The Young and the Restless*. I knew that if I took the talent I had on the stage and transformed it into film and TV, it could be my big success. The decision to turn my back on it was incredibly hard, but those avenues weren't fulfilling for me, and they weren't my path to alpha.

ZERO TO COCKSURE: A SLIDING SCALE

Being cocksure is an extreme end of the alpha scale. Cocksure is all external: bluster, showing arrogance, and all ego. Since I wasn't fulfilled in acting, I could portray cocksure all I wanted, but internally, I wasn't feeling like an alpha and I wasn't feeling confident. I was on the other extreme end of the scale, at zero. I needed to find my way to a balance point between zero and cocksure to feel like an alpha.

For a time, I shot boudoir photos in Los Angeles like it was going out of style. I constantly had beautiful women in the studio taking their clothes off to be photographed. Such work was powerful to me in another way. I saw women connecting with themselves and their own confidence in profound, moving ways.

I know my commercial boudoir and erotic photography online looked like I was always photographing actresses and supermodels, but that wasn't the case. I had clients who'd been through breast cancer treatments, women going through rough divorces, and all kinds of different backgrounds and life experiences.

Women would write to me all the time telling me how empowered, beautiful, and free they felt after getting their pictures taken.

They weren't just taking their clothes off; the experience allowed them to find their confidence and their freedom.

One client of mine told me that for 10 years she felt dead in her marriage. She said the experience of getting her pictures taken was so amazing and that it made her feel free and alive for the first time in years.

I helped these women connect with themselves and parts of themselves they thought they lost or they'd never connected with at all. One well-known actress did a boudoir shoot with me and said, "I hope you get paid a lot of money for this" because of how profound her own experience was. I loved the work, and I loved to see how transformational it was for my clients.

Even so, I was still questioning my purpose and unsure if photography was mine.

I had questioned my purpose so much by then that I knew I couldn't stop asking whether acting or photography or the focus on frequency was my purpose. The answer was always the same: mindset and conscious awareness. I needed to make both a part of everything I was and did. Acting and photography helped set the stage for a greater understanding of my purpose and what it means to follow it. Those journeys helped me expand on my thoughts and ideas about alpha, confidence, and mindset because I saw those concepts in action with my photography and acting endeavors. I studied them.

The more I got into the bigger messages I had about mindset and conscious awareness, the more I worried people wouldn't take me seriously if I was still taking boudoir or erotic photos. I thought to myself, "This isn't the kind of thing Tony Robbins does."

For me, there was also the concern of the societal perception of nude photography.

My fear was that nobody wanted to listen to a mindset coach who took nude pictures of women. How could I talk about mindset, masculinity, and alpha without anyone coming after me and calling me a hypocrite or attacking my photography work? As impactful as it was for these women on their own journeys to alpha, I wanted to ensure that no one would come after my messaging and call it bullshit.

It was important for my own alpha transformation to acknowledge that acting and boudoir photography were a part of who I was. Embracing that reality helped me come into my own and accept that I'm a bit of a misfit or motley crew type representation of mindset. I'm incredibly complex, and I'm there for the complexity in other people.

My journey was my real compass. It wasn't so much about what was going on in the world as it was about the internal discussions that I had with myself. To this day, I still have those conversations with myself in an attempt to remain conscious and aware.

I recently reconnected with a friend whose wife is a well-known porn star. When we first got to talking again, it took me a little while to get around her chosen career. Not because there's anything wrong with sex and nudity, but because there's a pop-culture, societal stigma around its existence that I had to acknowledge and consciously think past. Even I, a photographer who worked capturing nudity, can be conditioned to judge the tiers of nudity, sexuality, and the expression of it.

Finally, I reached the point with my friend where any judgment turned to, "You want your wife to be happy and if she's doing something she loves, great." Pivoting into that perspective allowed me to distance myself from his marital choice because part of being alpha is getting to the point where we are free enough to make our own decisions and be confident in ourselves without social media and pop-culture influences dissuading us from our truth. We have a lot in this world to think past if we are to truly tap into our alpha abilities.

TAPPING INTO YOUR ALPHA

The ability to tap into this gift is realized by pivoting into the perspective that the alpha is one of our most important brain waves. The alpha wavelength is the most present state of the mind. It is the meditative state and the bridge to our subconscious. It wields the ability to recondition our minds with any goal imaginable.

Few realize that we all are given the gift of being the alpha at birth and later purposefully using the alpha brain wave.

I didn't realize it either. In the very beginning of my online coaching journey, a business partner brought me to the concept of alpha. Before I made it into mindset coaching, I worked as a personal trainer, but it didn't make me feel like I could help people the way I wanted to. I dove into teaching meditation to kids and a lot of other self-development, which eventually led me to mindset coaching. I knew that I didn't want to sit directly across from someone in a room like traditional therapy because the statistics for therapists and suicide were staggering,[8] and as an empath, I wanted to protect myself. So, Prodigy Mindset was born, an online hub where I could provide mindset coaching, post videos, and help people without in-person interaction. A business partner I had at the time helped me get the ball rolling. He wanted me to train him and work with him while we were developing the brand. Something he wanted me to push was the idea of alpha. So, I needed to find out its origin before I could push it and promote it.

That point brought me to the alpha wolf myth.

Then, the concept of alpha brought me back to alpha brain waves; I had studied them briefly in the past but was now seeing them in a different light. I went back to studying things like YouTube videos about meditation with alpha beats and binaural beats. I did my research until I understood what the alpha brain waves felt like and meant. To me it's conscious awareness, moving past mental blocks for clarity. When you sit or move with intention and purpose, you get into the alpha state, or as I like to refer to it, the "runner's high." That's what the alpha brain wave provides. There's a buzz that we all catch when we put in the work.

Beta waves represent physical arousal, whereas alpha waves are slower with higher amplitude. Men and women reach an alpha state when they are resting and reflecting after completing a difficult task. Exercises like meditation, weight training, and yoga get

---

8 Tiffany Li et al., "Suicides of Psychologists and Other Professionals: National Violent Death Reporting System Data, 2003-2018," *The American Psychologist* 77, no. 4 (2022): 551–564, https://doi.org/10.1037/amp0001000.

you in the alpha state. Taking a break from your daily grind to take a walk in the park, enjoy a beautiful sunny day with birds singing and children playing and laughing, places you in the alpha state. Doing all of it consciously is the trick.

I like to relate alpha frequencies (8–12, etc.) to what spiritualists call manifestation. When men and women learn to tap into alpha brain waves with the purpose of manifesting, we align with our power and purpose simply by default; we become the powerful alpha by its only true and scientific meaning.

Meditation and quiet reflection aren't the only way to achieve that alpha state—which is a good thing because meditation doesn't work for everyone. Some people find it too slow; they get anxious from sitting still, or it isn't as mind-opening for them.

Part of the journey is discovering what alpha looks like for you. Is it meditating, running, painting? When you know how to get there, you can begin tapping into alpha regularly and removing mental blocks.

Alan Ritchson, who plays Jack Reacher in an Amazon Prime Video action series, has this whole "to the stop sign and back" concept."[9] He says that when he's feeling resistance to train, he tells himself to get out the door and just run to the stop sign and back. He just has to get out the door and do it.

Once he gets to the stop sign, he usually keeps going because he's

---

9   "Definitions," NeuroHealth, accessed March 7, 2024, https://nhahealth.com/
     brainwaves-the-language/.

hit the alpha brain wave, and all those mental roadblocks aren't there anymore. He has clarity and awareness.

What does it look like to tap into alpha?

One example is to not get up in the morning and immediately reach for anything digital. Do some kind of physical, creative, or relaxing activity instead. You most certainly shouldn't be thinking, "I need to get up, brush my teeth, and then meditate." What's important is not the thoughts about those actions; it's about curating the thoughts in between those actions with repetition and eliminating all the things that will trigger you and remove your connection with conscious awareness.

A man who truly understands the God-given power of his mind, is self-aware of his ego and his wants, manifests his life's purpose with a greater sense of ease, balance, and confidence. That state of mind takes the same level of practice and commitment that top elite athletes utilize to reach their full potential, which we will be exploring further in subsequent chapters.

THE POWER OF THE MIND

Tapping into alpha brain waves is the first step of understanding and navigating the power of the mind. Every human mind is incredibly powerful, but harnessing its power and using it for a higher purpose is complicated, difficult to learn, and has to be done over and over again to keep it going.

Think of the mind like a submarine. How many people know how to fully operate a submarine? It isn't a large number, I can tell you that. However, submarines are incredibly powerful and complex machines. Knowing how to operate one takes training, hard work, and gives the operator an advantage. On top of its existing complexities, new and updated technologies require continuous study and work.

The same is true for the mind.

A lot of people don't realize that it takes a long time to learn how to use the faculties of our mind. Every single day, no matter how good you get at it, you have to practice. I see all these quick fixes about "three-day manifestation courses" and "live your best life with these 10 steps." They are talked about as a quick, one-time solution to all the problems in life and toward helping you achieve your goals.

The soul journey is going to take a lot longer. It takes practice to tap into alpha and to utilize the power of your mind, and it has to be done as often as you would train the body. And you can't just tap into it, make your millions, and then retire on the couch. The journey never ends. If you stop the work too early, you'll experience what I call a spiritual sugar rush and crash—just like Johnathan "Johnny Football" Manziel experienced in his NFL career. As Johnny experienced, success that comes too easy and too soon loses respect for the process.[10]

Some people I've worked with start feeling really good after just a

---

10   Jaclyn Hendricks, "Johnny Manziel Sets Record Straight on Football Future After Fan's Dolphins Speculation," *New York Post*, February 1, 2024, https://nypost.com/2024/02/01/sports/johnny-manziel-sets-record-straight-on-football-future-after-speculation/.

few days, thinking they got what they need and stop the practice. Later, they come back to me and say, "I got there too soon." They realized after they stopped that there was more work to be done. Looking back and asking, "What the hell happened?" they realize they should have stuck with the work. It takes a lifetime to evolve.

You're always going to have a spiritual rush when you first tap into the power of the mind and if you don't keep up with the work, you're going to have a crash. I tell people all the time that they need to learn their crash patterns so that they can avoid getting trapped by them.

Knowing your whole self is key to reaching and maintaining conscious awareness; self-knowledge isn't just about one aspect of your persona. When I talk about the alpha mindset, I see it as a place of balance in mind, body, and spirit.

Not only is alpha status achievable but it is a duty to uphold. In order to achieve alpha, you have to do the work, understand alpha brain waves, and reach the culmination point of self-love, boundaries, and the understanding that all of us are connected. Society doesn't validate your alpha status. It has to come from within, your own self-love, self-respect through setting and maintaining boundaries, and conscious awareness of yourself and those around you. The correct and accurate definition of an alpha is a highly conscious being who is a beneficial presence to themselves and society.

CHAPTER 2

CRITICAL THINKING AND ALPHA BRAIN WAVES

Social media and news outlets have done a lot to warp the concept of alpha into a personality or a physical presentation.

Mainstream media labeled former president Donald Trump as the consummate alpha male. Writers for the *Telegraph* in the U.K. wrote in 2017 how he displays alpha-male body language, such as a "power handshake."[11] The *Guardian* described Trump as the peak of male physical prowess.[12] A Reuters report in 2018 made similar observations. It noted the handshake between Trump and North

---

11   Gus Kelly and Charlotte Krol, "Donald Trump's Alpha Male Body Language Tics—From the Hand Tap to the Power Shake," *Telegraph*, May 25, 2017, https://www.telegraph.co.uk/men/the-filter/donald-trumps-alpha-male-body-language-ticks-hand-tap-power/.

12   Don P. McAdams, "It's an Alpha Male Thing: What Dominant Chimpanzees and Donald Trump Have in Common," *Guardian* (US), September 14, 2017, https://www.theguardian.com/us-news/2017/sep/14/donald-trump-alpha-male-chimpanzee-behavior.

Korean leader Kim Jong Un.[13] A 2023 article for Leaders.com describes alpha males as ambitious, attractive, and high-status.[14]

I found it funny that Trump's "alpha" status was being determined by his powerful handshakes—especially since there's a lot about him that doesn't align with the true meaning of alpha. He's not alpha in the sense that he's not taking care of himself on the true alpha level. Alpha men understand that they are only as productive and successful as their minds and bodies are sharp and healthy, respectively. He may be bullheaded and push through shit, he might be smart and resilient against all the lawsuits and bullshit thrown his way, and he gets shit done. But he is too cocksure, too loud, too aggressive, and that's not leadership. As such, Trump is more aligned with Andrew Tate in the old-school version of alpha male.

Many years ago, I ran into "Stone Cold" Steve Austin in a restaurant. He was a professional wrestler in the WWE. At 6'5" tall, he's a massive powerhouse, and to become such a high-level athlete, he's needed discipline, determination, and an alpha mindset. Even if the WWE wrestling is a "setup," getting thrown around the way wrestlers do still requires being in top physical performance. You don't get to that level without being alpha.

When I shook Austin's hand, his handshake was so soft and almost timid. There was no conscious awareness put into his handshake.

13   Sam Holmes and Miral Fahmy, "'Alpha Male' Handshakes as Trump, Kim Meet, but Body Language Shows Some Nerves," Reuters, June 12, 2018, https://www.reuters.com/article/uk-northkorea-usa-bodylanguage/alpha-male-handshakes-as-trump-kim-meet-but-body-language-shows-some-nerves-idUKKBN1J806I/.

14   Jill Babcock, "The Alpha Male Archetype: Embracing Strengths Amidst Controversy," Leaders, August 9, 2023, https://leaders.com/articles/leadership/alpha-male/.

The same is true for Mr. Trump. Can it be said that Trump shakes hands consciously? Most likely not. He's not somebody who's very self-aware, which he displays in his actions often.

Ever since "Stone Cold" Austin shook my hand, I made sure that I didn't have a handshake like his—or Trump's for that matter. I made my handshakes a conscious act, ensuring each handshake was nice but firm, not too firm and not too aggressive.

To be alpha, there is a level of critical thinking and conscious awareness that comes from the alpha brain waves. When you tap into them, you can apply them to actions as simple as a handshake or to even larger, impactful actions.

The first step is understanding the true meaning of alpha and beta.

BETA WAVES FOR ALPHA MEN

Social-media users of all ages have likely seen or heard about the musical genre known as "K-Pop." The South Korean boy band BTS is the headline group for this genre and is extremely popular in Asia. Their shtick revolves around their physical appearances. The seven-member band looks very effeminate and androgynous. They wear lipstick and other heavy makeup on stage. These guys are considered "beta males" to the casual observer because they lean toward a specific image of soft masculinity.

Dictionaries define beta males as subordinate, passive, and subservient. Alphas are dominant, professionally successful, and sexually aggressive. Both of these descriptions are inaccurate and misleading. Alpha and beta are mental states of mind, not categories for men.

The human brain produces enough electricity (about .09 watts) to power an LED light bulb.[15] Brain activity is measured in cycles per seconds or Hertz (Hz). The slowest brain waves are theta and delta waves. These are present in sleep states. Gamma waves are the fastest, with frequencies up to 100 Hz. Many scientists, however, do not distinguish gamma and beta waves. Regardless, beta/gamma waves are the fastest in the human brain.

Beta waves are activated during normal consciousness. Routine work tasks, watching a movie, and surfing the web on your phone is beta mode. Logical thought and result-oriented tasks are beta activities. But too much beta leads to depression and anxiety due to overload and monotony.[16] Beta cannot be the primary wavelength for healthy, successful men and women. There has to be a balance with alpha brain waves, which is why being alpha is a state of mind that taps into brain waves.

ALPHA BRAIN WAVES IN MEN

Deliberate physical and mental relaxation define alpha mode. You're not thinking at a "high-performance" level or engaged in complex tasks. Listening to your favorite songs, cooking a gourmet meal, and reading an engaging book are alpha activities.

Our natural instincts and behaviors as human beings and men are active during alpha states.

---

15   "Your Amazing Brain," National Geographic Kids, accessed March 7, 2024, https://kids.nationalgeographic.com/science/article/your-amazing-brain.

16   "Neurofeedback: Train Your Brain Waves to Treat Anxiety, ADHD & More," NeuroHealth, September 26th, 2019, https://nhahealth.com/neurofeedback-train-your-brain-waves-to-treat-anxiety-adhd-more/.

Alpha brain waves are the second fastest in frequency. These frequencies create a detached awareness, similar to meditation, the runner's high, or doing yoga. Alpha waves represent intuition, particularly when you reach the lower limits around 7.5 Hz.

Alpha women tend to seek like-minded "alpha males" because they communicate spontaneously, both verbally and with body language, they're self-reflective, and they exist in balance on the zero-to-cocksure scale. For both parties, the courtship process is natural and enjoyable. Alpha men are natural fathers, husbands, and providers.

Similarly, corporations seek confident, decisive individuals for upper management. Intuitive thought is easily identified by Human Resources and recruiting staffs. Alpha brain waves are also associated with what is called a "sixth sense." Great inventions and ideas come during alpha states. Many great inventors and creatives say that the best ideas come to them when they are doing something as simple as taking a bath or looking up at the stars, not when they are focused on their work.[17]

To be an alpha in any field—personal life, career, romance—you first need to gain command of critical thinking. That objective means understanding conscious command between the alpha and beta wavelengths.

---

17   Richard Sima, "Why Do We Get Our Ideas in the Shower? The Science of Shower Thoughts Us the Importance of Mind Wandering for Creativity," *Washington Post*, January 12, 2023, https://www.washingtonpost.com/wellness/2023/01/12/shower-thoughts-creativity-brain/.

CRITICAL THINKING AND ALPHA BRAIN WAVES

Critical thinking has no universal definition. The general concept entails analyzing, evaluating, and applying facts while considering potential confounding variables. For instance, a hypothetical research question asks, "Does body weight and proportionality affect your ability to attract women?" The material answer is "yes," in most cases. But income and resources also affect attraction. Women, from an evolutionary standpoint, are more attracted to men with resources (a confounding variable). Thus, you cannot take the original poll question at face value.

Critical thinking is most often done on the brain's beta wavelength. You're typically in a beta state during normal daily activities—working your job, doing homework, working out at the gym, etc. Those high-level activities move fast to realize potential. The saying "haste makes waste" specifically relates to high-level thought.

Critical thinking is not being argumentative or attacking someone else based on their position. It's a process of identifying fallacious details, faulty reasoning, and biased information to reach a logical conclusion. The alpha state is relaxation, visualization, and peaceful consciousness. Your parents, teachers, and other mentors likely told you at some point to "sleep on it" before making big decisions. A critical thinker is one who diligently considers his conscious mindset at the time of important decisions.

The conscious mindset of the alpha frequencies get you the best thinking results. In order to refine the skill of critical thinking, you need to get into that creative flow that happens in the alpha state—in the shower, walking in nature, sitting at a red light. When you're in the conscious mindset, you get the flow from the alpha state that allows for better critical thinking in the beta state.

You need to prep in alpha to get into beta.

It's about stepping up to the plate in alpha. Consciously knowing you are doing something or are going to do something—such as calculations, high-performance thinking, work, social activities, etc.—is what will bring you into alpha before you take on that work.

If you don't, you're the athlete who didn't check themselves on the platform to achieve a great score on the dive into the pool. That's the athlete who is just a little off, thinking the one thought in the wrong direction. They aren't as conscious that day because they didn't consciously shift from alpha to beta ahead of time and then back to alpha before directing their attention to the task at hand.

If they don't come into themselves with conscious command and repetition of that alpha-to-beta-to-alpha cycle, they'll be a little off. You need to have moved consciously into alpha before you walk through those doors and consciously remain in alpha when you walk out of those doors.

One of the greatest enemies to critical thinking, and thus achieving the conscious mindset, is social media.

CRITICAL THINKING IN THE DIGITAL AGE

Social media and the internet have shrunk the world. At the same time, digital tools have widened ideological divide and atrophied critical thinking.

Pew Research Center tracked opinions on several issues and compared results over 23 years. There was an average 15 percentage-point gap between left-leaning and right-leaning individuals on all topics in 1994. That gap widened to 36 percentage points in 2017. Since the 2020 election and pandemic, the breach of divided opinions has most likely widened even further.

This phenomenon is glaring as it relates to opinions on the Coronavirus pandemic. A majority of left-leaning individuals (59%) believed the pandemic was a major public health threat versus 33% of right-leaning individuals. Most Americans overall (62%) believe news media have exaggerated and even fabricated coverage.[18]

Critical thinking is more important than at any time in our history due to the foregoing effects of social media and the internet. Unfortunately, that skill is rare in the 21st century, particularly among younger people. The 2019 "State of Critical Thinking" survey by Massachusetts-based MindEdge placed a spotlight on the gradual extinction of this important life skill.

The survey presented nine questions about fake news to 1,001 college-educated Americans. Most respondents (69%) failed

---

18   "Pew Research Center: Numbers, Facts, and Trends Shaping Your World," Library of Congress, accessed March 7, 2024, https://www.loc.gov/item/lcwaN0002821/.

the test, answering five or fewer questions correctly. The survey showed that critical thinking improves with age, finding that 43% of Baby Boomers (age 55+) passed the test with six or more correct answers versus 26% of Millennials (age 23–38). Granted the test excluded Generation X and is thus incomplete, but it provides a launch point for reinforcing a vital skill.[19]

When I browse through social media, I do it very consciously. Someone shared an interesting post the other day that I really liked. But they didn't share their sources, and I had no way of confirming that what they shared was factual. So, of course, I didn't like it or reshare it because I'm consciously aware that it might not be factual, even if I resonate with it.

In the same way that Donald Trump and "Stone Cold" Steve Austin shake hands without any conscious awareness, a lot of social-media users absorb what's thrown out on the platforms without considering the truth, reality, or impact provided by the content.

That lack of critical thinking on social media is how fake news gets spread around. Honestly, I don't even consider social media "social" anymore. It is more like voyeur media. It's people watching other people and not commenting or liking anything. Rapper and record executive Rick Ross made a great video questioning why he doesn't see people supporting their friends' posts. It's a valid question since social media was designed to connect people, but if all they are doing is watching, there's no real connection.

---

19   "MindEdge Critical Thinking Study Finds College-Educated Americans Fail at Digital Literacy," MindEdge, June 25, 2019, https://mindedge.com/news/mindedge-critical-thinking-study-finds-college-educated-americans-fail-at-digital-literacy/.

Almost everyone knows (or has been) the person who decides not to post certain pictures or events on their platforms because they told someone else that they'd be somewhere else and want to keep up that deception. It is a complete waste of brain power when that's what social media is being used for.

There's a common idea that social media has ruined us—that is, humanity. It is a dinosaur position because social media is here. The digital age is here. It's not going anywhere. We need to own it and work with it.

Once I accepted that truth, I no longer had those "critical thinking hang-ups" where I was thinking, "I need to keep this information from so and so." Sometimes transparency on social media is the best way to make it work for you.

When I injured my neck recently, I didn't disappear from social media. Instead, I posted about my recovery. I was transparent about the dominating part of recovery, wanting to push through the pain and make it back. I also was transparent about when I was falling apart because recovering from that injury wasn't easy, physically or emotionally.

During this process, I had people commenting on my posts and reaching out to me directly to talk about how they were going through a similar thing.

It could have been easy for me to disappear off social media, hide what I was going through, and then come back with some announcement post about how I took a break from social media but I'm back now and happier than ever.

I see the ruse all the time. Aspiring influencers disappear off social media when something heavy happens in their life. They try to hide their imperfections and only post about the happiness and perfect moments they have. It feels disingenuous, and it's all for the sake of voyeurism, not socialization.

The digital age is incredibly tricky, and it's here for us. There's something to be said for truth, honesty, and transparency for critical thinking in the digital age.

THE KAEPERNICK-JETS "SIGNING"

Society moves fast in the 2020s. We've turned into an instant-gratification species that is more concerned with finishing the task than doing it right.

The perfect example is when a Twitter (now X) parody account once tweeted that the New York Jets signed quarterback Colin Kaepernick to a one-year, $9 million contract. Many journalists, politicians, and other influential people reacted with a range of emotions, from praise to disgust. They ended up deleting their responses when it came out that the account that tweeted the news was a parody.

The "news" provided a simple critical-thinking moment that many passed up in favor of being first to react. It also proved the foregoing data: Critical thinking is a lost part of collective consciousness. Connecting with your alpha wavelength facilitates critical thinking in a world of boundless information and instant gratification.

Sadly, a lot of people rush to be first. That's part of our downfall in the digital age. As a photographer, I used to tell other up-and-coming photographers, "Don't get caught up in the content wars." Despite that great advice, I contracted the "virus."

KIN TO THE CONTAGION OF HERD MENTALITY

Around 2012 to 2013, I was getting published in fashion magazines with other photographers whom I admired very much. I was so stressed out every time I did another shoot. I was trying to keep up with the best of the best, those other photographers I kept seeing in magazines, and I constantly felt anxiety over it. I wasn't thinking critically; I was caught up in wanting to be the first to make it and in comparing myself to the other photographers.

When people rush to act first, they aren't thinking critically. Then, in a lot of cases like the Kaepernick parody account, people will go back and remove their comments when something turns out to be fake, or suddenly, their comment doesn't make sense. It is so important for them to have the "right" image of themselves that they dive in feet first on trending topics and then delete all association with it the moment the trends change. There's no truth and no critical thinking or conscious awareness behind their actions.

Our phones are another area that drain our critical-thinking skills. We are constantly overrun and saturated with our phones ruling our lives. Critical thinking becomes blocked when we are bombarded with constant demands for our attention. When we go through digital deprivation—stepping away from social media and other digital media platforms, outside of work purposes, for a set number of days—it helps reset our critical thinking. When I go back onto social media after 10-day digital deprivation stints, I'm thinking much more critically. When I realized how beneficial digital deprivation was, I incorporated into my programs, and the results that my clients experience with conscious command are transcendent.[20]

It is just like weight training. Digital deprivation is a training process on how to navigate the digital age. The gain from an absence produces the outcome that I have to critically think; therefore, "I don't want to like this content until I know you've done your research."

The digital world requires us to be reflexive, and that's where critical thinking ties in. Our relationship with the digital age must be reflexive—that is, adapting our reactions—to our own conscious command and critical thinking.

Conscious awareness equates to alpha brain waves; conscious awareness equates to critical thinking.

REPETITION TO TAP INTO ALPHA BRAIN WAVES

It's the repetition of affirmations that leads to belief.
And once that belief becomes a deep conviction, things
begin to happen.

— **Muhammad Ali**

Repetition is the key to unlocking alpha. When you run, your legs go in front of you and hit the pavement one step after the other—that's repetition. It eventually brings you to the "runner's high." You have to keep it going to get to that point. The same

---

20   Mathura Shanmugasundaram and Arunkumar Tamilarasu, "The Impact of Digital Technology, Social Media, and Artificial Intelligence on Cognitive Functions," *Frontiers in Cognitions* 2 (2023), https://doi.org/10.3389/fcogn.2023.1203077.

goes for repetition of thought: You have to keep the reps going to hit the "alpha high."

I first learned repetition and affirmation from Napoleon Hill's book, *Think and Grow Rich*. It's all about saying what you desire and knowing what you're willing to give in order to receive.[21]

I was put to the test when I was living in my car after a set of circumstances beyond my control put me in a houseless situation. When the temperature would get down below freezing, I would think about what I was willing to give to change my position. On top of it, I'd tell myself over and over again "I'm a tough son of a bitch. I'm a tough motherfucker." And I went to bed happy every night. It was the repetition of that thought, what I was willing to give, that opened my mind to conscious command.

I was also working on being grateful because there was a lot of greatness happening. My actions and ability to stay consistent in them while I was living in the car were providing me with a greater sense of confidence. To catch that process and gratitude in real time was powerful. That's when I learned that it's about the details.

HONOR THE DETAILS, AND THE DETAILS WILL HONOR YOU

All affirmations become stagnant. It's going to happen. That point is where most people drop off, but that's where the real work begins, where the real magic happens. For years I repeated the same

---

21   Napoleon Hill, *Think and Grow Rich* (Meriden, Connecticut: The Ralston Society, 1937).

affirmation about feeling "accomplished" and "successful" before going to sleep at night in my car. I was always needing to find new ways to reinvent and expand on those words to keep the feeling alive. It wasn't until I began focusing on tiny, tiny details that it really allowed me to unlock conscious command. I'd think, "An email sent out in a timely manner, sure, let's compound that thought and successful feeling!" If I could think of it, relate it, and celebrate it in my affirmation, I would. The time in terms of thought, creativity, reflection, envisioning, all hit that alpha frequency—the runner's high.

The tiny details truly are the most important. Take, for example, the work and commitment necessary to excel in professional sports. It is beyond comprehension for most people. The competition is against the best of the best. The most athletic and talented teams typically win at the collegiate level. That hallowed ground is hardly ever the case in the professional ranks. The details of a win are not always obvious. Look at the Los Angeles Lakers, which were heavy favorites against the Detroit Pistons in the 2004 NBA Finals. The Lakers, led by Shaquille O'Neal and the late, great Kobe Bryant, were expected to sweep the series and win their fourth championship in five years. The Pistons were simply hungrier and wanted it more. That's the tiny detail.

I felt like that Pistons team—I wanted it more. The same intensity that athletes put into their training, I put that into the reinvention and repetition of affirmation. I later found it was most powerful when I ate. Whenever I ate, I was full of gratitude and present. I also began fasting, which put me in a state of full gratitude and brought conscious awareness into my diet. In the moments leading up to eating, you start to become conscious, asking questions about what you should eat and if it is the right thing. By the time you start eating, you're already conscious. You're aware that you made your choice and the reasons behind it. With affirmation and repetition, it turned eating into an alpha experience. And it would help me discover the four best times to train in alpha. I made these training times a part of what we teach at Prodigy Mindset.

Likewise, that kind of repetition and subsequent discoveries helped me bring my visions to life. My creativity and production went up. Life got better all around. It's conditioning. The houseless situation allowed me to condition myself. It started to give me that "buzz" all the time, and I started meditating less because I was getting more via repetition of thought and affirmation. I was in conscious command. That state is where my understanding of the Internal Monologue System (IMS) came along and took my conscious command to a whole new level.

CHAPTER 3
SELF-TALK AND THE INTERNAL MONOLOGUE SYSTEM (IMS)

*If I finish a book a week, I will read only a few
thousand books in my lifetime, about a tenth of a
percent of the contents of the greatest libraries of our
time. The trick is to know which books to read.*

— **Carl Sagan**, *Cosmos*

The Internal Monologue System (IMS) is everything.

The IMS provided the answer to why I would find myself at the top of my metaphorical mountain while sitting in meditation, then easily triggered and spiraling out of control in my day-to-day moments. My Internal Monologue System bridged the gap and taught me what meditation couldn't.

Like many of us, I was an OG self-sabotager. Cream of the crop, baby! But that would end when I learned how to leverage my Internal Monologue System. Although the effects wouldn't be immediate, I was well on my way. I needed to have enough respect for process and repetition to fuel my IMS and my vision of who I wanted to be. Like in acting or in a movie script, I would need a character and words to bring my vision to life. I would need to invent Arlen J.

I like to say that my short-lived TV acting career was one of the worst and best things that ever happened to me. I went straight to producers in my first TV audition. After a quick meeting in the casting director's office, she walked me into a room and said, "This is my Isaac." Her words and tone indicated that there was no other option. She had already decided after seeing me perform in a play on stage that weekend. She called me in the following Monday, and I got the part before I left the building.

For a "newbie" to both the TV industry and self-development, it was the kind of quick confidence-to-success wake-up call I needed. The success that comes too easy or too soon risks losing its respect for process and repetition. I would learn that the hard way.

I had lived in Los Angeles just a few years before my instant success, but opportunities had me exiting quickly to spend some time in Vancouver, British Columbia, and in Chicago, Illinois. I had a strong desire to live in different cities long enough to find a routine. To me, it seemed more transformative than traveling. I had the spirit of a vagabond. So, of course when my mother called me, crying in 2003 because she was diagnosed with Leukemia, I once again hit the road to Corpus Christi, Texas.

I wanted to help however I could. My time in Texas was transformative. I meditated 1–3 hours a day, got back into resistance training, and dieted accordingly. I had never read much, but I was starving for non-fiction. I read the *Road Less Traveled* by M. Scott Peck, M.D., and the world went from black and white to color. I quickly developed a sense of ease and power that I never knew existed. I was putting in the work and learning to believe in myself like never before. Then it hit me: I had been unconscious of creating so much unnecessary adversity in my past, and that thought terrified me. I was awake now.

I thought, "Shit, am I about to die? There couldn't be anything more important to learn in this world than conscious command. This is eye-opening shit; I must be done for!" That thought process was short-lived, and I was feeling limitless by the time my mother went into remission a year and a half later. Los Angeles kept coming to mind when I questioned where I wanted to go and what I wanted to do with my new sense of power. In addition to having been an athlete, I was a stage actor in high school and college.

I felt confident in translating that skill set to the screen. I had a great "bad guy" look and knew I could leverage it. Back it up with the bulletproof routine I had going—what could go wrong? I hadn't been in L.A. for more than a year when a mentor told me, "Arlen, the career is there for you if you want it." If I want it? His words hit like a ton of bricks. I hadn't questioned if I wanted it. Not well enough, anyway. I then realized my motivation for self-development had been heartache. I wanted to be seen by the people I was trying to prove myself to, and TV would do that.

Any goal or purpose driven by fear, heartache, lack, and limitation has a way of coming back to haunt us. It was hitting me all at once; I had just committed to 10 years in L.A. What the fuck do I do now?

I had no actual practice in getting hit and getting back up. That shock to my ambition was the first big blow since embarking on self-development. Then, I got advice from a fellow actor that really struck me. He said, "Don't put a life up on the screen until you've lived one yourself." There it was; building the characters on the page took me away from the work I had been putting in with my own character.

I was within balance on the zero-to-cocksure scale when I put my own character's self-development at the helm. I was all alpha, and that frequency quickly opened doors that I wasn't ready to handle. I couldn't see my crash patterns coming, and it shook me to the core. It was clear that my self-sabotaging subconscious stories were far too dominate to spend time on any character other than my own. I knew I would destroy myself in front of everyone if I continued as an actor, and that consequence would be hard to bounce back from. I also knew that I was on to something bigger.

As an actor, I was only as confident as the amount of time I put into building that character and the words that character spoke. What I put in is what I got back. It would take some time to harness this insight, but I proved how to transform my own character through thoughts, words, and a respect for process and repetition. Putting in the work—like an actor would from page to stage—is a good example of the focus and effort it takes to keep self-sabotaging stories at bay and achieve greatness. That combination would shape my understanding of the Internal Monologue System (IMS).

THE IMS SUMMED UP AND IN ACTION

From time to time, I get the opportunity to sit down and talk mindset with some incredible entrepreneurs, athletes, thought leaders, and creatives of all kinds.

I had the pleasure of speaking with other actors and actresses who were far more successful than I in that field. The reason I never reached that success was because I didn't have the kind of desire, belief, or confidence they had in that area, the same confidence Retta described when I had the pleasure of interviewing her while she was filming the TV show *Parks and Recreation.*

What was supporting her and costar Amy Poehler's confidence? It was the IMS.

During the interview, I asked, "Was there ever any doubt in your decision to become an actor?"

Retta replied,

> I think about how Amy [Poehler] and I were sitting in the makeup chair. I can't remember how we got into it, but we were both talking about how we just knew that it was going to happen for us. We were never stressed and thinking, "Will I ever make it?" "Will I ever be a working actor?" My thing was *when.*

If someone could just tell me when, then everything would be good. And for Amy, she was like, "I'm going to do Second City, and then I'm going to be on SNL." She wasn't thinking, "God, I hope this Second City thing works out and that people like me enough that hopefully I get to audition for SNL." Instead, she thought, "I'm going to do this so I can do that." "And because I'm doing this, I'M GOING TO DO THAT." That's not necessarily everyone's route. But Amy decided that it was her route, and it was going to happen. It's about having these thoughts in your head. And maybe I created it in my head, knowing that I needed it if I was going to do it.

Comedy Central has a stand-up competition called Laugh Riots. And I did it back in '99. If you won, you got a car. You also got to do a spot on their Premium Blend. So, I did this semi-final thing out in La Brea and won. The day before the finals, I was driving in my terrible '84 Mustang to meet my friend and her sister for dinner. I remember thinking, "God, I can't wait to get rid of this car when I win tomorrow."

Actually, what I was really thinking was "what am I going to do with this car?" because I was going to win, and I was going to get rid of it. The conviction about the next step was really weird and kind of a matter of fact. So now, when things come to me in a manner of "so, what do I do when?" and not "what do I do if?" I know whatever it is, is going to happen. My body has accepted that it is going to happen. My brain has accepted that it is going to happen.

> And as proof, there were some funny people in that show,
> but I won. It's not like every day I think this way, but I do
> have those moments.[22]

Retta's words about thinking it and making it happen perfectly sum up the power of the IMS as a form of self-talk manifestation.

LEV VYGOTSKY: A BRIEF HISTORY ON THE FATHER OF SELF-TALK

The IMS is directly related to self-talk. The concept is one that a lot of people are familiar with, but where did self-talk originate? Soviet revolutionary and politician Leon Trotsky is credited with being the father of self-talk. He was staunchly anti-capitalist. He believed social classes cause perpetual struggle. His goal was to end such divisions with Marxist principles. He believed social classes inhibited conscious connection and turned people into servants of materialism.[23] His views on the foregoing, which he called "reshaping of man" were summed up in his 1924 work *Literature and Revolution*.

> Man will make it his purpose to master his own feelings,
> to raise his instincts to the heights of consciousness, to
> make them transparent, to extend the wires of his will
> into hidden recesses, and thereby to raise himself to a new
> plane, to create a higher social biologic type, or, if you
> please, a superman.[24]

---

22   Retta (comedian and actress), in discussion with the author, 2011.

23   Robert V. Daniels, "Leon Trotsky: Russian Revolutionary," *Encyclopedia Britannica*, last modified November 3, 2023, https://www.britannica.com/biography/Leon-Trotsky.

24   Leon Trotsky, *Literature and Revolution* (1924; New York: Russell & Russell, 1957), Trotsky Internet Archive, accessed March 7, 2024, https://www.marxists.org/archive/trotsky/1924/lit_revo/.

Lev Vygotsky used that quote in his 1926 doctoral dissertation called "The Psychology of Art." He concluded said dissertation with a quote from Dutch philosopher Baruch Spinoza:

"That of which the body is capable has not yet been determined."[25]

Trotsky and Spinoza shaped many of Vygotsky's theories, particularly his focus on self-empowerment.

Today's athletes, like Michael Jordan, Tom Brady, and LeBron James, could very well be the "superhumans" that Trotsky and Spinoza referenced. Those individuals represent humans who have those high-performance levels.

Vygotsky was born in Belarus in 1896, which was then part of the Russian Empire. He was admitted to Moscow University in 1913 where he studied medicine for a year before transferring to law school. Vygotsky never earned a degree there because the Bolshevik Uprising in 1917 disrupted his studies. He became a prominent representative of the Bolshevik government in Gomel (Belarus) thereafter.

The Psychological Institute of Moscow invited him to be a research fellow in 1924. Though he completed his aforementioned unaccomplished Ph.D. in 1926, it was not published until sometime in the 1960s. Vygotsky died of tuberculosis in 1934 at age 37. But by then he had made his marks in philosophy, politics, and psychology, particularly as they relate to the concept of self-talk.[26]

---

25   Lev Vygotsky, *The Psychology of Art* (Cambridge, MA: The MIT Press, 1974), https://www.marxists.org/archive/vygotsky/works/1925/index.htm.

26   Kendra Cherry, "Lev Vygotsky's Life and Theories," Verywell Mind, last modified February 22, 2023, https://www.verywellmind.com/lev-vygotsky-biography-2795533.

VYGOTSKY CIRCLE AND SELF-TALK

Vygotsky first explored self-talk as a psychological concept in the 1920s. His work is often cited as foundational research in the realms of cognitive development and social development theory. Russian neuropsychologist Alexander Romanovich Luria was establishing himself at Moscow University's Clinic of Nervous Diseases at that same time. He was a preeminent researcher on various types of neurosis. Vygotsky and Luria teamed up in 1925. The two men set out to understand "elementary" and "higher" mental functions in both adults and children.

A highly influential network of scientists, educators, and doctors became Vygotsky collaborators. They expanded on his work from the late 1920s until the beginning of World War II. The group incorporated Vygotsky's theories into their own work and further flushed out concepts related to social and interpersonal relations.

The Vygotsky Circle was integral to the development of Soviet science. The group was particularly interested in childhood development. The consensus was that children needed one vital tool to become self-regulated adults. That postulation was the beginning of positive self-talk. The Vygotsky Circle sometimes referred to it as "private speech" or "inner speech."[27]

The concept has evolved and changed throughout the decades, leading me to discover the importance of the IMS and how it can

---

27   Róisín Flanagan and Jennifer E. Symonds, "Self-Talk in Middle Childhood: A Mechanism for Motivational Resilience During Learning," *Psychology in the Schools* 58, no. 2 (2021): 1008–1025, https://doi.org/10.1002/pits.22484.

be used to change thought patterns and gain control of your life and purpose.

ALPHA BRAIN WAVES AND THE IMS

The law of attraction, in the simplest of terms, means you manifest what you think and envision. Thoughts become reality. Your thoughts affirm your life and existence. You attract what you want your life to be. If you're consumed with thoughts of being a failure or underachiever, that image is what your life will be in perpetuity. If you are poor and stuck at a job you hate, you will remain poor and miserable until you change your thought processes.

The universe won't help. It cannot decipher a good person from a bad person. It cannot make a good person good and a bad person bad. When good people, in standing for justice, continually emote the frequency of injustice, they manifest injustice. It's the law of attraction. Angst begets angst. Composure emotes calm and ease. Conscious men and women are aware of that very slippery slope. They are prepared to respond. They don't react.

Everything in our being can be broken down into subatomic particles and energy waves. Those particles, however, aren't out there on solo missions. Everything is interconnected and influences the energy around it. Earth's energy field is like a giant interconnected network, like the internet. Each human, animal, plant, etc., is like their own website with individual energy, but also connected to the web as a whole.

We are energetic beings. We vibrate at varying frequencies. The brain interprets these frequencies like a powerful transceiver. It decodes frequencies and repackages them into everyday stimuli that are picked up by our eyes, ears, taste receptors, etc. A combination of your IMS and the alpha wavelength facilitates the manifestation processes.

When you bring the IMS and alpha brain waves together, you gain conscious command of your own reality. If you want to eliminate negativity from your life, you can manifest that outcome. If you want to stop arguing with your significant other, you can manifest that, too.

COUNTERING NEGATIVITY WITH THE IMS

Emma Young, an award-winning science and health journalist, is one of many experts who agree that 95% of brain activity is outside of our conscious awareness.[28] The late Dr. Emanuel Donchin put the number even higher:

> An enormous portion of cognitive activity is nonconscious. Figuratively speaking, it could be 99 percent; we probably will never know precisely how much is outside awareness.[29]

Human beings, at least those in the Western 21st century world, are naturally wired to harness negative energy. Past research showed that the human brain has anywhere from 50,000 to 80,000

---

28   Marianne Szegedy-Maszak, "Mysteries of the Mind: Is Your Unconscious Making Your Everyday Decisions?," U.S. News & World Report, February 28, 2005, https://faculty.fortlewis.edu/burke_b/personality/Readings/AdaptiveUnconscious.pdf.

29   Daniel Goleman, "New View of Mind Gives Unconscious an Expanded Role," *New York Times*, February 7, 1984, https://www.nytimes.com/1984/02/07/science/new-view-of-mind-gives-unconscious-an-expanded-role.html.

thoughts per day, while new research says we have approximately 6,000 "thought worms" daily. Not only are about 80% of those said thoughts negative but also are the same negative thoughts from the day before. It could be an insult that hurt your feelings from 20 years ago or the food tray you dropped while working your server job last week. Whatever the case, it's easier to dwell on negative thoughts.[30]

Similarly, the pain from a stinging insult is far more powerful than someone saying that you look nice today. The cliché "You never get a second chance to make a first impression" was born from the foregoing phenomenon. Negative first impressions are stored in our brains more vividly and are more easily accessible than their positive counterparts.

Some blame this phenomenon on negative conditioning from toxic interactions and programming from social media and television, respectively. But there is no denying that the phenomenon exists. Take the studies of the late University of Chicago professor Dr. John Cacioppo. He showed test subjects photos that arouse positivity (e.g., a pizza, a graduating student, etc.), negativity (e.g., a dead cat), and neutral feelings (e.g., a fork or spoon). He monitored electrical activity in the brain and found a much higher surge when the brain received negative stimuli.[31]

---

30 "New Study Suggests We Have 6,200 Thoughts Every Day," Big Think, July 16, 2020, https://bigthink.com/neuropsych/how-many-thoughts-per-day/; Crystal Raypole, "How Many Thoughts Do You Have Each Day? And Other Things to Think About," Healthline, February 28, 2022, https://www.healthline.com/health/how-many-thoughts-per-day.

31 Hara Estroff Marano, "Our Brain's Negative Bias," *Psychology Today*, June 20, 2003, https://www.psychologytoday.com/us/articles/200306/our-brains-negative-bias.

The negativity bias is especially bad for men because it causes unnecessary stress and anxiety. Stress causes blood vessels to constrict, while the body redirects blood to the limbs to prepare you for battle. The effect leads to all kinds of ailments, including heart disease, obesity, and erectile dysfunction.

The negativity bias is an omnipotent force of our minds if we allow it to be. It takes conscious effort to combat it. When we commit to curating our own IMS in the way that professional athletes practice free throws, route running, and swinging a bat, we self-induce a heightened state of alpha brain wave consciousness. Self-talk as a discipline promotes neural plasticity, which helps the brain to reprogram itself and eliminate subconscious, detrimental habits and mindsets. If made to be reflexive, positive self-talk can protect and accelerate a man's mindset at will.

Therefore, if you understand the alpha mindset and make your IMS reflexive, it doesn't matter what confusing or detrimental "alpha male" concepts are floating around in today's media. You'll have the conscious command to sidestep negativity and self-sabotaging thoughts and live a healthier life.

That advantage includes overcoming fear and other negative emotions that we use to self-sabotage and hold ourselves back.

FEAR KILLS DREAMS

Fear of failure is one of the most common reasons that people don't start their own businesses. Data compiled by the *Global Entrepreneurship Monitor* in 2018 found that 33% of Americans feared starting a business.[32] The fear of leaving a stable 9–5 job with benefits prevents millions of people from pursuing what they've always wanted to do because failure means you may not have that security blanket job waiting for you in the aftermath.

The entrepreneurial spirit is more robust in younger people, particularly men (Gen Z and Millennials) because they don't want/need college educations and student loan debt. Regardless, fear does not discriminate based on age. Sir James Dyson, best known for his Dual Cyclone bagless vacuum cleaners, once said, "The key to success is failure. Success is made up of 99% failure." It took him over 5,000 prototypes to perfect his signature invention and propel him to billionaire status. Every successful man has an anecdote or quote summarizing how they overcame fear and became successful.[33]

J. Ivy is among those ranks. Twice I interviewed the talented poet, songwriter, author, and 2024 Grammy Award winner. He made a profound statement in one of the interviews related to aspirations and reaching for your goals: "Dreams don't come true; they are true," Ivy said. He was referring to performing with Kanye West and Jay-Z while recording the Grammy Award-winning song "Never Let Me Down" in 2002. Ivy told *Billboard* in 2014 that he didn't believe the opportunity was real when producer Coodie (of Coodie and Chike fame) offered it to him. His reaction was, "Stop bullshitting." But the opportunity was real. Ivy

---

32   Niels Bosma and Donna Kelley, "2018/2019 Global Report," *Global Entrepreneurship Monitor* (2018), https://www.gemconsortium.org/file/open?fileId=50213.

33   Thomas Shambler, "The Key to Sir James Dyson's Success (Despite 5,127 Failures)," *CEO Middle East*, December 8, 2016, https://www.ceo-middleeast.com/ceo/business/the-key-sir-james-dyson-s-success-despite-5-127-failures-655595-html.

performed his verse over the phone a few days later, and the rest is history.[34]

There is nothing unhealthy or antisocial about fear. Millions of men across the globe are God-fearing men. Many of their peers hold them in high regard despite a 12% drop in Christian-identifying Americans from 2009–2019. Dr. Theo Tsaousides, writing for *Psychology Today* in 2015, said fear is healthy. Fear is normal. It is not a sign of weakness. Fear is hard-wired in every human being. It must be leveraged, not eliminated, Dr. Tsaousides wrote. J. Ivy understands that concept.[35]

"Fear, stress, and anxiety will stunt your creative growth," he said. "You must constantly remind yourself of that mental fortitude, spiritual fortitude, and just stay conscious and aware of where you're at and where you're going."[36]

Like most successful men, Ivy has achieved and sustained conscious command for most of his adult life. He said that riding his bike and writing are two activities that have an effect similar to meditation on him, bringing him the runner's high. Ivy naturally gets to the alpha brain wavelength because he was shy as a kid with little self-confidence. He became a deep thinker as a result. His early grasp of conscious command helped him manifest his dreams into reality.

---

34 Raquelle Harris, "J. Ivy Talks About Being the Grammy-Winning 'Poet Who Sat by the Door,'" *Billboard*, April 6, 2023, https://www.billboard.com/music/rb-hip-hop/j-ivy-poet-interview-grammy-win-1235298895/.

35 Theo Tsaousides, "7 Things You Need to Know About Fear," *Psychology Today*, November 19, 2015, https://www.psychologytoday.com/us/blog/smashing-the-brainblocks/201511/7-things-you-need-know-about-fear.

36 J. Ivy (poet, songwriter, and author), in discussions with the author, 2011 & 2020.

"Even in the conscious world, we have the ability to construct how we want to maneuver and move forward," he said. "If you don't deal with your emotions, your emotions will deal with you."[37]

As we all know, learning new skills, especially when it comes to emotional regulation and reprogramming the mind, is a lot harder after reaching adulthood. By then we are pretty set in our ways. That's why I compare my mindset journey to that of a professional athlete. The rigorous training, discipline, and commitment were required for me to make those changes in my life. What if it didn't have to be that hard?

SELF-TALK IN MODERN ACADEMIA

Today, in many psychology and philosophy programs, self-talk is incorporated into the curriculum. Newer and more modern theories about self-talk are being utilized in academia versus the original research of Vygotsky-Luria. Yet, no specific chapters or sections in the most commonly utilized textbooks for undergraduate psychology address self-talk as a distinct subject matter.

Self-talk is used more as a therapy taught to students to maximize their academic potential in the 21st century. Researchers in Madrid, Spain acknowledged that the concept of self-talk gets very little attention in academic psychology, similar to the conclusion by American professors. But these same researchers performed an experiment on 177 University of Madrid students in their first year of psychology studies. The experiment measured their levels and types of self-talk and subsequent academic performances.

---

37   J. Ivy, in discussion with the author.

Students reported more negative than positive self-talk when faced with difficult forthcoming assignments. Those who reported more positive self-talk about forthcoming difficult assignments obtained better academic results than those who reported negative self-talk. Those who reported negative self-talk performed very poorly or failed.[38]

Researchers believe that the negative self-talkers projected negative images of themselves, and that ideation materialized in their actual performances. Researchers, however, concluded that those who suffered from negative self-talk could have performed better with professional intervention or even by speaking about their concerns with other students in order to redirect self-talk in a more positive direction.

Positive self-talk is, for whatever reason, discounted as a scientific field of study in 21st century academia. Dr. Paul Karoly, professor of psychology at Arizona State University, stated that books and articles are often written about internal speech and its relevance to motivation, learning, and psychopathology. But he said self-talk as a discipline is mostly observed as assessments administered to college students to measure their confidence levels.[39]

I believe that in order to change the collective mindset and have positive self-talk be as prevalent as negative self-talk, the concept needs to be introduced at a much younger age. Tapping into the IMS should be reflexive, and if it is presented to kids in preschool/elementary

---

38   Flor Sánchez, Fernando Carvajal, and Carolina Saggiomo, "Self-Talk and Academic Performance in Undergraduate Students," *APA Psychnet* 32, no. 1 (2016): 132-147, https://doi.org/10.6018/analesps.32.1.188441.

39   Paul Karoly (professor of psychology, Arizona State University), interview by researcher for ArlenJ.com (unpublished), 2018.

school and taught about it and how to use it, they will have much better tools going into high school, college, and adulthood.

The psychology students who are being introduced to self-talk at the college level aren't having the same "aha" lightbulb moments that allow them to use the IMS in their careers or teach it to their clients and patients in the workforce. At least, not for all of them. Imagine how much different your high school and college years could have been if the IMS and positive self-talk were already reflexive by the time you reached that age!

Integrating the IMS into an academic curriculum for young children and students wouldn't be that complicated. It isn't an entire new course of study. Instead, each school day could start with a top-of-the-morning IMS practice. After that initial prep, each transition from one subject or event to the next could be made smoother by taking a step back, working with the IMS, and reconnecting to conscious command before moving forward. It's about getting the students to become conscious of moving from alpha to beta via the IMS.

It's that easy!

Children's minds are overflowing with activity and creativity. Trying to slow them down with relaxation and meditation is almost a disservice to their development and to unlocking the power of the mind. It is that kind of thinking that leads boys and young men to grow up fearful of pursuing their dreams, their purpose, and their passions. If we can connect them to the alpha mindset and IMS, teaching them positive self-talk, self-awareness, and conscious command, they won't be so fearful. They'll trust themselves and their manifestation power to create their own success and reality.

CONSCIOUS OR UNCONSCIOUS, HUMANS ARE PROLIFIC THINKERS

While children's minds in particular might be bursting with activity and creativity, all human minds are constantly working and thinking, whether you're conscious of it or not.

The heart beats approximately 100,000 times a day.[40] Breathing happens about 20,000 times a day.[41] And blinking occurs approximately 21,000 times a day.[42] Just like a heartbeat and breathing, thoughts happen automatically, making them a type of bodily function. While the heart, lungs, and blinking can be left up to unconscious behavior, our thinking cannot. The National Science Foundation estimates that the average person has around 6,000 "thought worms" per day. The thinking mind is a prolific bodily function that must be consciously curated to excel in our purpose. And just like those same bodily functions, thinking doesn't have to be—and shouldn't be—unconscious.

While the main purpose of blinking is to moisten our eyeballs and protect them from debris, we have the ability to consciously blink

---

40   "How a Healthy Heart Works," Heart&Stroke, accessed March 7, 2024, https://www.heartandstroke.ca/heart-disease/what-is-heart-disease/how-a-healthy-heart-works.

41   "Breathing," Canadian Lung Association, accessed March 7, 2024, https://www.lung.ca/lung-health/lung-info/breathing.

42   Allie Johnson, "Blinking: Frequency and Why We Do It," All About Vision, April 13, 2022, https://www.allaboutvision.com/eye-care/eye-anatomy/how-many-times-we-blink-per-day/.

whenever we want. However, even when we aren't consciously aware of it, blinking still happens.

Likewise, our heart beats automatically. We don't have to concentrate to make it happen. And yet, there are breathing techniques and other thought-intensive practices we can perform to consciously slow down our heart rate. With them, we can control our heartbeat.

Thoughts are the same. They will happen unconsciously, but you can still tap into them and gain control of them the same as with blinking and your heartbeat.

Thoughts are made up of memories, visions, emotions, and can trigger our Internal Monologue System just as our IMS can trigger our thoughts. If leveraged, our prolific thinking can help curate our IMS. Think about your thoughts like running water. You don't want to stifle it, stop it, or even slow it down. You want to shape it, direct it, and clear the path so it can continue flowing forward. By using the IMS to shape and direct thoughts, and vice versa, we help generate and sustain the alpha frequency.

CHAPTER 4

SELF-TALK AND SPORTS PERFORMANCE

Professional athletes and top sports performers are perfect examples of how to use the IMS and be a high-performance thinker. You can't be successful long-term in sports, or any field, without incorporating self-talk, the alpha mindset, and conscious command. Those components are necessary to balance the scale of zero to cocksure and reach that superhuman performance level.

Likewise, timing is everything when it comes to releasing movies and books. The ESPN/Netflix miniseries *The Last Dance* continually set rating records as new episodes premiered. It was a right place/right time scenario as all sports had been halted since late March 2020 due to the COVID-19 pandemic. Of course, I was right there watching the show along with everyone else.

As great of a story as it was, I found it lacking, sadly, as it glossed over some of the most important aspects of sports performance.

The series chronicled the career of NBA Hall of Famer Michael Jordan. It particularly focused on Jordan's last season in the NBA. Many sports journalists and pundits consider Jordan the greatest basketball player of all time and rightfully so. The 10-episode series included interviews from 90 people, ranging from basketball greats like Magic Johnson and Larry Bird, to Carmen Electra and former president Barack Obama. There was one surprising and incomprehensible exclusion from the interviewees: George Mumford.

THE FORGOTTEN GURU OF MICHAEL JORDAN'S SUCCESS

Mindfulness is the state of being conscious. Cognition is the brain process for acquiring and understanding knowledge and experiences. Mumford has studied both for more than 35 years. As author of the book *The Mindful Athlete: Secrets to Pure Performance*, Mumford started his own journey toward a permanent positive mindset after a life-changing event. He was a basketball player at the University of Massachusetts and roommate of teammate Julius Erving (a.k.a., "Dr. J").[43]

Mumford suffered major injuries that forced him out of the game. He became addicted to prescription pain killers and eventually moved on to heroin. Mumford ultimately enrolled in Dr. Jon Kabat-Zinn's Mindfulness-based stress reduction program. He got off drugs, earned his master's degree, and began teaching mindset training to others.

---

43   "George Mumford: Keynote Speaker," Chartwell Speakers, accessed March 7, 2024, https://www.chartwellspeakers.com/speaker/george-mumford/.

Mumford was brought in by former Chicago Bulls head coach Phil Jackson in 1993, two years before Jordan returned to basketball. The team was in disarray after Jordan "retired" to play baseball. Mumford's job was to teach players how to deal with the anxiety and pressure that comes with both success and failure. His website says it all about his relationship with Jordan:

> **"Michael Jordan credits George Mumford with transforming his on-court leadership of the Bulls, helping Jordan lead the team to six NBA championships."**[44]

The Last Dance documentary told the story of Jordan's personal trainer talking about how Jordan needed to bulk up to beat the Detroit Pistons. It said the trainer also changed Jordan's routine to prepare for baseball. One could say the series overestimates the importance of physical attributes over mental training. The term "mind over matter" is somewhat cliché. But science says there is a lot of truth to it. We see it all the time in sports, specifically in the area of self-talk. A mindset coach like George Mumford is paramount to pro-athlete success because his methods help pros tap into the IMS and alpha mindset.

A lot of pro athletes get there on their own or with the help of family and teammates. There is a certain amount of conscious command and alpha brain wave activity that leads to that kind of success in the first place. However, with the true greats—the superhumans—mindset goes beyond their natural abilities.

---

44   "'The Mindful Athlete' Book," George Mumford (website), accessed March 7, 2024. https://georgemumford.com/the-mindful-athlete-book/.

George Mumford helped Michael Jordan become a basketball legend instead of just being another great NBA star. He guided Jordan through mindset coaching and self-talk. It seemed like the documentary glossed over an important personal topic because Mumford truly is an unsung hero in the career of the greatest basketball player ever.

SELF-TALK: IN THE WORDS OF PRO ATHLETES

The mental game is what separates the good players from the great players.

— Aaron Judge

There are countless examples of self-talk contributing to the success of some of the greatest names in sports, music, and other high-profile careers. A well-known example of self-talk is Muhammad Ali. He didn't just say it to himself, he told it to everyone who would listen.

Muhammad Ali is the most famous positive self-talker in history. Not only did he tell you, "I am the greatest fighter in the world," on a regular basis, but also went out and proved it with the same frequency.[45] Many of the greatest athletes of all time literally talked their ways to greatness.

The Utah Jazz Hall of Fame big-man, Karl Malone, used to say something out loud at the free-throw line before releasing the shot. Nobody understood the words he was saying at the time. But "The Mail Man" made only 48% of his free throws as a rookie and 60% his second year. He knew those numbers had to improve for him to become,

---

45   Alex Trickett, "When Clay Shook Up the World," BBC Sport, February 24, 2004, news.bbc.co.uk/sport2/hi/boxing/3516241.stm.

arguably, the greatest power forward ever. With his own brand of conscious command, Malone shot below 70% on free throw only once from his third year forward—69.4% in the 1993-94 season.[46]

Keith Henschen, a sports psychology professor at the University of Utah, worked as a consultant for the Utah Jazz in the 1980s and 1990s. He revealed in 2002 that Malone sought Keith's help early in his career. Malone was saying, "This is for Kay [his wife] and the baby," according to Henschen.[47] Speaking those words prepared Malone mentally to make free throws.

Tennis fans know that self-talk is ubiquitous in the sport. Eight-time Grand Slam Singles champion Andre Agassi provided a first-hand explanation as to why so many professional tennis players talk to themselves out on the court.

> *Tennis is the loneliest of sports. In golf, you play the course—plus you have a caddie—and the game ends at 18 holes. In boxing, you have a corner man and a set number of rounds. In tennis, you're on an island, with no clock. You can't sit on a lead. You have to win the last point to win a match. You're out there, you can't talk to anybody, you can't pass the ball, there are no time-outs. There's no coaching, you don't have to be good, you have to be better than one person and that person is on the other side of the net.*
>
> **— Andre Agassi**

---

46   "Karl Malone," Basketball Reference, accessed March 7, 2024, https://www.basketball-reference.com/players/m/malonka01.html.

47   Michael Bar-Eli, *Boost!: How the Psychology of Sports Can Enhance your Performance in Management and Work* (New York: Oxford University Press, 2017), 258.

What Agassi was saying is that it takes self-talk to rev up tennis players in order to perform at their highest levels. They only have themselves to rely on and only their IMS to guide them.

Pete Sampras won 14 Grand Slam Singles Titles in his career, fourth all-time in the men's bracket. He held the world No. 1 ranking for 286 weeks, second only to Roger Federer. Positive self-talk was a big part of his success. Sampras was known for saying aloud motivational things like, "I need to let go of that last point and focus on the next point," while on the court. "Everything is okay," was another frequent phrase Sampras used for positive self-talk.[48]

If you're thinking that positive self-talk is exclusive to professional sports, think again. These are examples of some incredibly successful individuals who understand the power of the IMS and how it contributes to their success. But the IMS is beneficial to everyone and can bring you the same levels of success and high performance as professional athletes—in your own life and career fields.

SELF-TALK AND SPORTS PSYCHOLOGY (CONTEMPORARY)

There is no question that positive self-talk impacts performance in virtually all competition, whether that's your career, sports, courting a love interest (which is a sense of competition, trying to prove yourself the best option over everyone else), academics, etc.

---

48   Gary Bala, "Tennis Self-Talk: Historical Examples and Solutions," Essential Tennis, accessed March 7, 2024, https://www.essentialtennis.com/tennis-self-talk-historical-examples-and-solutions/.

In one example, high school seniors were instructed to use instructional and motivational self-talk while performing accuracy and distance tasks related to throwing a softball. These athletes performed distinguishably better than another group who were instructed to use unrelated self-talk.[49]

The so-called 1970s cognitive revolution in psychology was the point when sports psychologists began focusing research on self-talk and its effects on performance. These early studies in self-talk and sports psychology were mostly based on the 1957 work of Albert Ellis and his Rational Emotive Behavior Therapy; along with Aaron Beck's 1975 Cognitive Therapy.[50]

Cognition became the focus of sports psychology versus the previous focus on personality during the 1970s. Negative self-talk is just as powerful as positive self-talk when it comes to sports performance. We often hear, particularly in professional sports, how a team quits on their coach. That breach essentially amounts to mass negative self-talk and very poor performance on the field of play, resulting in lopsided losses and coaches getting fired.

Those examples bring us to the self-invoking trigger hypothesis. It posits that subjects made to access their self-schema are negatively impacted in learning and performance tasks. The instant experiment asked participants to think about their past

---

49   Yu-Kai Chang et al., "Salf-Talk and Softball Performance: The Role of Self-Talk Nature, Motor Task Characteristics, and Self-Efficacy in Novice Softball Players," *Psychology of Sport and Exercise* 15, no. 1 (2014): 139–145, https://doi.org/10.1016/j.psychsport.2013.10.004.

50   Tadhg E. MacIntyre et al., "Editorial: Mental Health Challenges in Elite Sport: Balancing Risk with Reward," *Frontiers in Psychology* 8, no. 1892 (2017), https://doi.org/10.3389/fpsyg.2017.01892.

performance (self-schema) before embarking on a throwing experiment. A control group was given no such instruction. The group that activated their self-schemas performed worse on subsequent tasks than the control group did. A similar approach was taken with wiffleball tasks. The group that was told to think about their past results performed worse in the hitting tasks on subsequent days.[51]

This hypothesis is demonstrated on NFL and college football fields all the time with defensive backs. The adage goes that these players must instantly forget about being "burned" on the previous play and get right back to doing their job in covering the wide receiver. The best defensive backs have the shortest memories when it comes to failure.

The Last Dance documentary might have overlooked Michael Jordan's mental game, but top athletes never do. Many successful players shepherd conscious command with a well-curated IMS. This kind of reflexive self-awareness is known well by many champions.

> *I think self-awareness is probably the most important thing towards being a champion.*
>
> — **Billie Jean King**

We all are responsible for the quality of our own self-awareness and the self-talk that we generate at any given moment. When we

---

51   M. Yamada et al., "Do Attentional Focus Cues Affect the Type or Number of Explicit Rules? Proof of Concepts of the Self-Invoking Trigger or Explicit Knowledge Hypotheses," *Psychology of Sport and Exercise* 70, no. 102547 (2024), https://doi.org/10.1016/j.psychsport.2023.102547.

disengage from actively curating conscious command, we become vulnerable to self-talk derived from outmoded low-frequency subconscious programming. It's a risk that champions avoid, as do purpose-driven men and women.

THE THIRD-PERSON MINDSET AND SELF-HONESTY

I wanted to do what was best for LeBron James, and what LeBron James was gonna do to make him happy.

— LeBron James

Many athletes like Shaquille O'Neal, Cam Newton, Floyd Mayweather, and LeBron James have referred to themselves in the third person when speaking of their abilities and desires. The practice was labeled "egomania" by one journalist.[52] But what elite athletes like LeBron James utilize, consciously or unconsciously, is called "psychological distancing." It is the art of stepping away from an immediate identity and any possible pitfalls for a better view of the bigger picture. Consciously understood and implemented, speaking in third person can provide oneself with a secure pedestal.

Your inner speech should have an elevator pitch in the form of a third-person affirmation. The third-person mindset is what helps curate the IMS for high-performance thinking.

---

52   Amelia Ahlgren, "5 Reasons Shaq and Other Athletes Refer to Themselves in the Third Person," Bleacher Report, February 21, 2012, https://bleacherreport.com/articles/1075379-5-reasons-shaq-and-other-athletes-refer-to-themselves-in-the-third-person.

Those great athletes weren't using "I am" affirmations in those statements. Anyone who tends to come from a self-sabotaging place shouldn't start with "I am" affirmations. Instead, they should be taking inspiration from the pro athletes using third-person speech.

I consider "I am" affirmations more advanced work because it is easy to tell yourself that you are something or are going to do something, but without proper conscious command, the statement can quickly turn into lying to yourself. What happens is that those simple "I am" affirmations become hard work against your body and nervous system.

Neuroscientists discovered that the brain works harder when it is telling a lie than when it is telling a truth. They also found that just four parts of the brain are active during truth-telling, whereas seven parts are active during lying. In studies, this difference in brain states made it harder for subjects to perform a small physical task while telling a lie.[53]

Thus, subjects had a harder time performing well on the task of holding their arm up while their brains were busy telling a lie, compared to when their brains were engaged in telling the truth. Consider the same for affirmations and mantras. "I am always successful" is an example of a first-person affirmation. The nervous system will not support the statement if the statement fails to be true.

Your subconscious knows it isn't true, no matter how many times you say it to yourself. However, if you use psychological distancing

---

53 Noa Ofen et al., "Neural Correlates of Deception: Lying About Past Events and Personal Beliefs," *Social Cognitive and Affective Neuroscience* 12, no. 1 (2017): 116–127, https://doi.org/10.1093/scan/nsw151.

and that third-person mindset, the shift in perspective is enough to ease the resistance to your body and nervous system.

Back when I was trying to make my career as an artist, I had alternate sources of income to support myself. I was struggling as a bartender and server, constantly telling myself, "I'm a great photographer," or "I am making it as a photographer."

The problem was, I didn't really believe what I was telling myself. I was trying to tell myself that I'd already reached the end result by being this "thing." It sounded like complete bullshit because it didn't align with my life circumstance.

I had to find a different kind of affirmation that would amplify me and rev me up so I could reach the end result I wanted rather than lying to myself about who and what I was currently. That realization led me to the third-person mindset and the affirmation I began using to get me in that mindset.

"(Fill in Full Name)______________ is an accomplished, successful, well-respected, continuously sought-after, thriving, expansive (Fill in Desired Affirmative Statement) ______________."

I'd start my affirmation with my name. "Arlen J." Then I bring in two fuel words, "is an accomplished, successful…" Accomplished and successful being the fuel words that fired up the rest of the affirmation.

Back then, it was, "Arlen J is an accomplished, successful, well-respected, continuously sought-after, thriving, expansive photographer."

Now that I've done the work, I can adjust that affirmation depending on what I'm gearing up for. If I want to reconnect with my roots, I'd use the name James Arlen O'Keefe. Or if I'm trying to connect to my brand, I'll use the name Arlen J. The ending to the statement in the affirmation changes too.

The way I look at it, you have to learn to walk before you can run. Third-person affirmations are walking, building up your strength, getting in touch with your IMS, and cultivating repetition, reflexivity, and conscious command.

Again, the third-person statement creates less resistance from the nervous system.

FUEL WORDS AND REACHING THE FINISH LINE

I start my third-person mindset with "accomplished and successful" because they are fuel words. They provide tangible meaning and momentum for the rest of the affirmation. Those first two words are ones every person needs to get intimate with. You can be an accomplished and successful parent, CEO, student, soldier, etc. The words can be applied to anything and anybody.

Contrary to popular belief, it won't take someone into an egotistical place. A monk can be an accomplished and successful spiritualist and acknowledge it without bringing in their ego. It is a truth of who and what they are.

Fuel words are the words that kick things off. They "fuel" the mindset and the affirmation. When we say "accomplished and successful," we allow ourselves to look at the details of everyday life. When I talk about accomplishment and success in my third-person affirmation, I am focused on the small accomplishments and successes that I experience every day. Just as I mentioned in chapter 2, if you honor the details, the details will honor you.

If your focus is on the big-picture goals and ambitions, the smaller details will slip right by, and you won't recognize them. You lose respect for the process and the small details. It happens to all of us more often than we think.

A buddy of mine followed my program and told me that, "I guess I'm learning that happiness is a choice." The program taught him that. I thought, "Damn, that's an accomplishment." I provided him with the mechanics. That's an accomplishment for him and for me, even though it was such a simplistic moment between us. Looking at such moments, I can recognize their enormity. Accomplished and successful is about the small accomplishments and the small success.

Bringing those little details into your affirmation ensures that you bring in gratitude for yourself and the little, daily achievements. When you do it in the third person, you're amplifying your nervous system—that is, being consciously aware of the nervous system and that resistance is high performance. Respect for process, repetition, and the details brings in the realization that there's so much good to compound. And then you will realize that good is because you're creating it.

Since you've amplified your name with accomplished and successful, you've elevated your nervous system, making those words concrete, motivating yourself. They are fuel words, though, which means they kick things off. They won't get you all the way to the finish line. You need additional horsepower to get you there.

That point is where "well-respected, continuously sought after, thriving, expansive" come in. The next term in my affirmation—well-respected—comes in when you start to feel the details of being accomplished and successful from your fuel words. The result is that you start to do things that bring in respect, that get you up off the ground and start moving toward a place where you'll be sought after. It's a chain reaction of events.

In the ALPHA PRO program, our 21-day mindset initiative program that elevates conscious command and conscious creativity, one participant started training in the third person and realized he had been lying to himself. He realized he wasn't reaching what he wanted and that he wanted so much more than he was telling himself he wanted, making each day a struggle because he was living his own lie.

Once you get comfortable with that third-person mindset and affirmation, you can advance into "I am" statements that are true, and you can share them externally.

Going back to Muhammad Ali always saying, "I'm the greatest boxer in the world," you can't have the external without the internal first. Muhamad Ali had a pristine IMS. He felt it internally to the point where he felt it inside and out, and everybody else heard it, too. People believed him because he said it with confidence and proved it in his actions. He believed it to be true and that made others see it as true, too.

That effect is the difference between IMS internal to external versus someone who's bullshitting and lying to themselves. When the IMS is strong enough to come out, it's believable, it's confident, and you know it's true. When someone is using their voice to bolster themselves and make others see them a certain way, or trying to convince themselves something is true, it isn't as believable. It's like an actor who hasn't put in the work.

Most athletes will operate from internal to external because having a pristine IMS is what gets them to the level of success where they are big enough and confident enough to believe and to embody what they think to the point their spoken mindset becomes external for the rest of us to see.

THE STOKER MINDSET

It's not what you're capable of, it's what you're willing to do.

— Mike Tomlin

Part of the IMS and third-person affirmation is the stoker's mindset. When newcomers get introduced to my affirmation, I always imagine a stoker in a train or a ship shoveling coal into the furnace. And that's what you have to think like when you're curating those thoughts. You're going to get dirty, get primal. You don't have the right clothes, but you're going to dive in anyway.

A man I worked with said, "It really gets you tapped into this primal sense of conscious awareness," when he started using my affirmation. To me, the "primal" aspect is the stoker's mindset. Whatever reason stokers have for doing that job, there are no hang-ups. They are doing the most basic, underrated job to keep the entire machine running.

I tell people all the time that they have to fuel themselves, just like with those fuel words. Whether they think it is beneath them or ridiculous, they're going to shovel that coal until they can fuel their words and get themselves revved up. You have to start with the fundamentals before reaching higher.

A lot of people who come to me have reached too high and skipped over the fundamentals, or they forgot about the fundamentals when success came to them. Even professional athletes respect and understand the importance of those fundamentals. There is an idea that competitive basketball players make 500 hundred shots a day. These shots are fundamentals of the sport and encourage players to practice the basics so they don't overlook the hard work that got them there or need to do to stay at the top.[54] The other drive behind 500 shots a day is that all players have rivals. Better players who don't want to be outdone will be thinking about their rivals and the fact that they most likely got their 500 hundred shots in that day.

Once you start honoring the fundamentals, you'll get into the IMS and make it reflexive, amplify awareness, and reach new heights.

---

54   "How Many Basketball Shots Should I Take a Day?," Hoops Addict, August 7, 2023,
       https://www.hoopsaddict.com/how-many-basketball-shots-should-i-take-a-day/.

PRO-ATHLETE SELF-TALK FOR NON-PRO ATHLETES

I like to use self-talk in sports performance as a tangible example of the power of the IMS and the greatness it can help people achieve.

I once worked with a CEO who was making six figures a month. He reached that success quickly and once he got there, he lost his respect for process and repetition. He was enjoying life, and when you enjoy life, you can easily forget all the fundamentals.

Consequently, he lost his self-awareness. He was living by his ego and cocksureness. When life smacked him upside the head, his IMS wasn't set up and he wasn't well-prepared.

I started working with him, but he couldn't immediately wrap his mind around the IMS and alpha mindset. We simplified it, starting with the fundamentals and the stoker mindset. Then, after some digital deprivation, he realized how much clearer he was thinking.

That's when I told him, "Yeah, that's your IMS working for you." From there, he took off again, rebuilding his foundation and fundamentals.

In another case, a casting director I knew in L.A. ended up doing the program, and he told me he had an out-of-body experience while honoring the details with IMS repetition. He was above himself looking down on his life and being shown all the things he had. He stated that it almost felt like he was being pulled away. He wanted to go back because he could look at it all with absolute appreciation and gratitude, which IMS and repetition bring.

He said, "You get so caught up in high-performance success that it outstrips your gratitude for what you already have and what you've already created."

His film won an Oscar that year, and he felt that a lot of his recent journeys and our discussions helped get him to that point.

Another client had been trying to play guitar forever. Every New Year, he tried to make a resolution to learn guitar. From the time he was 18, he tried to do it every year and never could. In his 40s, he joined the ALPHA PRO program and learned to play guitar and wrote a whole country album.

He sent me a rough song of him playing guitar and singing that he had recorded on his phone, and it was fantastic. It blew me away. He was already an established singer/songwriter, but he had been a vocalist only. He'd never played guitar like that before. With conscious command, and respect for process and repetition, he was able to make that transition.

He told me how the process impacted him. He said, "The IMS really puts procrastination to the side." When you see your story of limitation, you have no choice but work around it. Because of his vocal success, he'd procrastinated learning guitar. He kept putting it off, like he didn't need it, and it was easier to put it on the back burner.

I do the same thing all the time. Sometimes, I get to a certain level of success and then realize I'm lagging in another area because I had all my focus in a different place.

With the IMS, you can reinvent yourself in any new area. Conscious awareness plays a key role in this reinvention process. It helps you sort through the questions: Do I need new ideas, or can I reinvent myself with what I already have? Are things so stagnant that I can't even get them off the ground?

To better understand the IMS, the alpha mindset, and conscious command, I've studied how high-performance sports legends implement it and credit it with their success. Self-talk is a powerful tool that can be applied to any aspect of your life, and with repetition and reflexivity, it can help you reach the same greatness as pro athletes.

CHAPTER 5

MAKING YOUR IMS POSITIVELY REFLEXIVE THROUGH REPETITION

You likely have had a doctor test your reflexes with a tap on the knee. Reflexes make the leg jump when the little rubber hammer is tapped in just the right place. It is an example of a human reflex—an unconscious reaction to external stimuli.

We are reflexive beings…whether the reflex is physical or behavioral. The word reflexive means to come back to oneself, like circling back around. Reflexive behaviors and thought patterns follow that circle.

Scientists have gained knowledge about the nervous system and how it holds the bigger picture of trauma we experience. They have learned that if some new trauma arises in life, even if it is a lesser experience than the original trauma, the nervous system unconsciously reacts to it as if it were the original trauma. It is a reflexive response because the nervous system holds onto that original trauma.

The same is true with the IMS. It holds the bigger picture of our behavior patterns and responses. If we can override those areas and get the IMS reflexive and positively charged, it can change reflexive responses to trauma patterns. Trauma isn't about getting into the root of it. It is about writing a new story within the IMS.

From day one of our lives, we begin to store experiences and events in our nervous system and subconscious. Over time, they build up and start to inform our responses. If traumatic, those same experiences are stored in the IMS and inform how we talk to ourselves.

The more we hear the same things through the IMS, the more we lean into those thoughts. If your IMS is always telling you that you're the greatest boxer in the world, like Muhammad Ali, then you lean into that feeling and that mindset. But if your IMS is storing trauma and always telling you that you're in danger, you're going to feel anxiety and paranoia.

That repetitive thinking eventually becomes subconscious, making it a reflexive response you don't even have to think about or can control. The good news is that through conscious command and repetition, you can retrain your IMS, rewire your thought patterns, and supercharge your nervous system.

UNCONSCIOUS REFLEXIVITY

The subconscious mind is just a reflex system. We're creating new reflexes and new experiences based on our reflexive responses. We are becoming more and more reflexive going in certain directions, where we spend most of our time. If we spend most of our time in trauma, that's where reflexivity takes us, unless we use repetition to change that mindset.

Sometimes, when we are still in our trauma, or the experience is very fresh, we might need additional help from a therapist or psychiatrist. Such individuals have an outside perspective to help us see things from a different angle. Once you've been shown that different perspective and move up through the stages of trauma, it is up to you to do the work on retraining your IMS so that you don't get trapped in your trauma again.

> *We are, each of us, largely responsible for what gets put into our brains, for what, as adults, we wind up caring for and knowing about. No longer at the mercy of the reptile brain, we can change ourselves.*
>
> — **Carl Sagan, Cosmos**

In my youth, I spent a lot of time thinking the worst. Whether it was my health or thinking something horrible was going to happen, my mind went to the worst places. Sometimes, I felt like I couldn't think of anything positive. So, I became more and more reflexive toward those negative, doom-and-gloom thought patterns.

It wasn't until I had this big "aha" moment that I realized what I was doing. Oddly enough, the revelation came from witnessing my mom's reflexivity. I watched my mother get stuck in this reflexive negativity all the time. She would be going through tons of turmoil, her internal IMS spewing negativity, her external voice constantly negative. She was living in anger, frustration, and complete anguish. And then there'd be this moment of silence after she worked herself exhausted and fell into a blank state. In that moment, she forgot about her problem and what she was upset about. Instead of dropping her anguish, though, her IMS again went into reflexive negativity. It's almost like the mind reached back to remind her what she was upset about, which starts the whole process and feeling over again.

I saw my mom in that state over and over. First, she couldn't remember what she was upset about, and then she'd be upset that she couldn't remember what she was upset about. Reflexivity kicked in, and she kept letting it in until it circled back around and became reconnected to what she was originally upset about, just dredging it up over and over.

I saw myself in the same cycle too. Once I was aware, I was tuned-in to the moments when I saw myself lose my negative thread. Instead of looking to trap it, pivot, and fuel forward, I tried to pick the negative thread back up again. I was asking, "Where's my problem at?" Even when I was detached from my problem, I was looking to get it back! That's insanity. Once I had conscious command, I could see what I was doing. Just because I could see this pattern didn't mean I was strong enough to override it. Conscious or not, that pattern was a reflexive beast to take on.

We can get addicted to our negativity. In remembering how my mother had this sense of satisfaction in finding what she was upset about after losing her thread for a moment, I also saw where I had learned this behavior. I knew I had to go to work to change it.

When you've lived in trauma, you become reflexive to search for trauma. You can have beautiful, peaceful moments but not enjoy them because your reflexivity is steeped in trauma. If you don't practice being peaceful, your mind tries to bring you back to what it knows—in this case, trauma.

That rubber band is going to come back on itself if we are not consciously curating a new story and making that new story reflexive, reconditioning the subconscious mind, working in alpha brain waves, using the IMS and all its components, and constantly being saturated in that process.

Unfortunately, the majority of us will experience some form of trauma in our lifetimes. If you're a person coming from trauma and you have lofty goals but have never been able to get there, then it's most likely because you're still living in reflexive trauma. Your will to lean into conscious command hasn't been strong enough, long enough.

> *Life rewards those who stay strong enough, long enough.*
>
> — Jesse Iwuji

REPETITION TO RETRAIN THE IMS

Reflexivity is unconscious, but repetition is conscious. Repetition leads to reflexivity because it creates new neural pathways and trains the IMS for good or for ill.

Floyd Mayweather, American boxer and boxing trainer, used a somewhat unorthodox training method. He'd be out partying at a club and after a night out, he'd pull sneakers from the trunk of his car and run home. He's made that training reflexive by doing it so many times, so he'll do it no matter what situation he's in. He has built neural pathways through repetition to support his training habits.[55]

Distractions always abound. My son, for example, is a competitive swimmer. He had a moment at a pool recently where he didn't have something he felt he needed in order to get his laps in. He just couldn't do it under those circumstances, and it got in his way. I used to be the same way when going to the gym. If I didn't have my specific gym attire on hand, I'd be groaning to myself, "Oh man, I have to go home and change and get my stuff." By the time I got home, I just stayed there. I wasn't going back to the gym. I'd already lost.

I wasn't fully aware that kind of thinking was negative or that conscious command could change it. If you're already unconscious to the proper mindset—whatever the source of procrastination—you'll never achieve your objective. You need conscious command.

---

55   Jack Figg, "Running Club Inside Floyd Mayweather's Unique Training Regime Including Running Back from Nightclubs in Jeans and Workouts at 4am," *Sun* (U.S.), November 13, 2022, https://www.the-sun.com/sport/758952/floyd-mayweather-unique-training-schedule/.

In this world, we find ways to make positive reflexivity so complex. "You've got to have the perfect workout gear, got to have your wraps, got to have this and that." It's not about that. It is about getting out there and doing it under any condition. Mayweather made himself reflexive under any condition to be able to throw on those running shoes and get his workout in.

It shouldn't matter what you have or don't have. You should just go out there and get it done. A lot of people are waiting for the perfect scenario to do the work. All too often I heard my mother say, "Oh, as soon as this happens, I'm going to do that." How many people walk through life saying, "As soon as this happens, I'll be happy," or "Once I get through this week, I'll have time to relax."

It's always one thing after the next after the next. People themselves fuel that vicious procrastination cycle, looking for the perfect scenario. I can't tell you how many times I've rolled up to the gym in just my jeans. I've worked out often like that, regardless of how silly or strange it might look. I knew that if I had that moment of "I should go train, but…" I had to stop there before finishing the thought. It was time to just go and do the training before I talked myself out of it.

Sometimes, I have to be very conscious of choosing to do whatever that thing is (go to the gym in jeans) regardless of how it looks. That kind of reflexiveness is what's going to get me there and help me keep my fitness goals.

That's how I retrained my IMS and my thought patterns. With conscious command, I created a new neural pathway for myself to be able to go to the gym under any circumstance, and that's where the great champions like Mayweather, LeBron James, and Michael Jordan, live. That's what, I believe, Mayweather was providing: a great example of how to train and beat opponents reflexively.

After a while, the repetition of commanding myself to go to the gym at the moment I felt like I should train stopped being conscious repetitiveness and became unconscious reflexivity.

Making your IMS positively reflexive is a way to elevate yourself to a high-performance lifestyle. Whether you're playing professional sports, running a business, or working a summer job, like lifeguarding.

I went to a Six Flags amusement park recently and brought the kids to the water park. I sat by one of the main pools watching the kids swim and have a good time. At some point, I looked at the lifeguards and every single one, in unison, were bobbing their heads, slowly turning in one direction. Then, they'd pause, and in one long line, sometimes with the aid of their hand tracing the pool edge, they'd bring their head back to where they started and began the process all over again.

I'd never seen that behavior before. I went and talked to one of the grounds employees who said it is a 10-second count. One, one thousand, two, one thousand… all the way up to 10, and they have to check their whole area in that 10-second span before going back to the beginning because it only takes 10 seconds for someone to drown. They have to cover the whole perimeter.

Sometimes, the Six Flags management will send a staff member in to fake drowning in those areas, and the lifeguards have to get to them in those 10 seconds. If the lifeguards miss a certain number of those saves, I think it's two, then they are fired.

That's high-performance lifeguarding. It's following the conscious command of repetition. They took on a job where they have to bob their heads and count to 10 over and over again. It sounded right on point because that's what high performance is. It looks so small, neurotic, stupid, and excessive, but if those lifeguards weren't willing to accept that job as anything more than kicking back on the lifeguard stand, blowing the whistle, and tanning, then they wouldn't make it.

Having to count and be in the moment like that takes commitment and willingness to do what other people won't. It's what makes them great.

It seems simple, but it could literally mean the difference between life and death in that situation. And we all should be the same with our goals. That one tiny thing, that one tiny moment could ruin us, like the 10-second window for someone to drown.

At any theme park or amusement park, there are so many people, so many distractions. To be able to shut all that out and just focus on counting and doing their jobs takes a lot of mental discipline, willingness, and repetition, and that commitment turns into reflexivity over time. It becomes an automatic response under those circumstances.

That power of repetition can be applied to your own actions and behaviors in any situation. It starts with the IMS, retraining your thoughts from negative to positive and creating positive neural pathways. Once that training becomes reflexive, it is much easier to shut out negativity, just like the lifeguards shut out distractions.

NEURAL PATHWAYS AND BEHAVIOR CHANGES

Theories on how long it takes to form new habits and change mindsets have been around for decades. Plastic surgeon Dr. Maxwell Maltz said in the 1950s that patients typically took 21 days to get used to their new noses after rhinoplasty. The same timeframe was noticed when patients received prosthetic limbs as a result of amputation. Dr. Maxwell's book *Psycho-Cybernetics* sold more than 30 million copies, with the primary thesis around the 21-day rule.[56]

Malcolm Gladwell, five-time *New York Times* best-selling author, is also well-known for his habit-forming theories. His most popular book, *Outliers: The Story of Success*, posited the 10,000-Hour Rule. Anybody wanting to achieve expert, world-class expertise in any industry is said to need 10,000 hours of practice and repetition.[57] Herbert Simon and William Chase's paper published in *American Scientist* magazine in the 1970s observed chess experts, including grandmaster Bobby Fischer. The authors concluded it takes 10,000 to 50,000 hours to be great at chess.[58]

Researchers have worked tirelessly to both debunk and confirm all these habit-forming mindset theories. A 2009 study published

---

56   Maxwell Maltz, *Psycho-Cybernetics* (New York: TarcherPerigee, 2015).

57   Malcom Gladwell, *Outliers: The Story of Success* (New York: Back Bay Books, 2011).

58   Herbert A. Simon and William G. Chase, Skill in Chess: Experiments with Chess-Playing Tasks and Computer Simulation of Skilled Performance Throw Light on Some Human Perceptual and Memory Processes," *American Scientist* 61, no. 4 (1973): 394–403.

in the *European Journal of Social Psychology* found that it took an average of 66 days for someone to form the habit of eating fruit for lunch.[59] The *British Journal of General Practice* defines a habit or mindset as "actions that are triggered automatically in response to contextual cues that have been associated with their performance."[60] For instance, in the COVID-19 era, many people automatically put on masks without thinking about it before leaving their homes.

The one thing all these studies and books have in common is repetition.

"You cannot teach an old dog new tricks," according to U.S. folklore. What if those words are not entirely true? The truth is that repetition ultimately becomes habit.

Another expression, "It's just like riding a bike," epitomizes how neural pathways are created. The first few times Dad took you out on your bike, you fell down, cried, and got back up. Once you mastered the ability to keep your balance and pedal, your brain saved that knowledge, like a computer hard drive. It's the same thing with driving a stick-shift car after 10-plus years not driving one. The neural pathways are instantly accessed whenever necessary.

The brain connects neurons with dendrites (nerve cell extensions) when it recognizes a habit or behavioral pattern. The more that

---

59   Phillippa Lally et al., "How Are Habits Formed: Modelling Habit Formation in the Real World," *European Journal of Social Psychology* 40, no. 6 (2010): 998-1009, https://doi.org/10.1002/ejsp.674.

60   Benjamin Gardiner, Phillippa Lally, and Jane Wardle, "Making Health Habitual: The Psychology of 'Habit Formation' and General Practice," *British Journal of General Practice* 62, no. 605 (2012): 664–666, https://doi.org/10.3399/bjgp12X659466.

behavior is displayed or the activity is performed, the more dendrites are produced. For example, when you move to a new city, you'll likely take a few wrong turns and not know exactly where you're going. After a few trips to and from work or home, you no longer need the GPS. The brain forms neural pathways when the activity is done repeatedly. Processes becomes faster and more efficient.

Dr. Deann Ware, a Dallas-based psychologist, wrote that brain cells' communication and strength of connection are positively correlated. "The messages that travel the same pathway in the brain over and over begin to transmit faster and faster," she wrote. Virtually all behaviors can become automatic with enough repetitions—free throws, typing, playing an instrument, etc.[61]

The creation of those neural pathways through the repetition with the IMS leads to high-performance thought and a high-performance lifestyle.

> *Winning is not a sometime thing; it's an all the time thing. You don't win once in a while; you don't do things right once in a while; you do them right all of the time. Winning is a habit.*
>
> — Vince Lombardi

HIGH-PERFORMANCE THOUGHT

There is no right or wrong time to train. There is no right or wrong time to fight. There's only winning all the time and working all

---

61   "The Neuroscience of Behavior Change," StartUp Health, Medium, August 8, 2017, https://healthtransformer.co/the-neuroscience-of-behavior-change-bcb567fa83c1.

the time, under any circumstances. I feel like I put 15 years into the IMS to the point where I'm doing pretty good. Would I like to be better? Yeah, I would. I came from such a mucked-up subconscious program with an incredibly messed up IMS. My baseline was very low. Manic depression, anxiety, and self-sabotaging behaviors. Where I'm at now is high performance to me, based on where I came from.

For you, high performance doesn't have to look like what I've described about some of these athletes. The scale of "high performance" is going to look a little different for anyone, based on their baseline. Regardless of your baseline or your high-performance state, it comes down to having that hunger and that willingness to create that Mayweather mindset that, under any circumstance, you're all in.

I had the wonderful opportunity to interview Super Bowl champion and three-time pro-bowler, Simeon Rice. We discussed his success and his mindset to reach that success. He talked about it being obsessive. Sometimes when our goals are so great, and it's going to take a lot to reach them, if you aren't obsessive, you're never going to reach that stage.

Simeon said,

> Before you have perspective of your surroundings, you have to have an introspective of yourself. I knew no one was going to outwork me. I knew that. It's not what I'm just thinking, I know. I would be in our facility building all night training. I know nobody's willing to do that. I

know I'm obsessive with that. I'm normally the first in and the last one out. That's just a part of me....

In life, when you don't suffer repercussions, people don't really have an ability to self-reflect because there's no penalty for it. You've got to be all in. But not a lot of people are all in. Because it's severe, it's obsessive, it's crazy almost, you know. I used to train my teammates, and they'd say, "Sim, I want to be an all-American; I want to be all-pro. I'm going to come out and train with you."

They would come out and 2-3 days in they're like, "Simeon, I can't do this, man." I've heard this before. "I want to be that good; I want to be on your level but I don't want to do all of this." I'm like "Then you don't want to be on my level." It's more blood, sweat, and tears—it's not as eventful as the event. It's not as flattering as you think. There is nobody screaming for you, the crowd isn't screaming your name. This is the prerequisite to having your name become famous. To have your name in lights. To have every kid rocking your jersey at the games. Prior to that, you have to be willing to go into the abyss.[62]

His combination of the IMS and his near-obsessive repetition with training gave him the unconscious reflexivity to surpass his peers and reach his major goals. I do the same thing now, still training at the gym at 2 a.m., long after other people have thrown in the towel.

---

62   Simeon Rice, interview by Arlen J, "Simeon Rice Interview: Revisit and Recommit," Prodigy Mindset, March 29, 2022, https://www.prodigymindset.com/post/simeon-rice-interview.

A lot of really smart, intelligent individuals, geniuses, great thinkers are out there who work hard, but they are not professionals of thought. Just like the other athletes who trained with Simeon and gave up when it became too rigorous and intense, those who won't master the necessary discipline don't reach their life's purpose. They aren't obsessive. Sure, it can be a conscious choice to lean into a lifestyle of balance, but if you still have dominant internal stories of lack and limitation, trauma, or self-sabotaging behavior at the helm, then the remedy is to want to fall in love with being obsessed.

Magic Johnson, a well-known pro basketball player whose given name is Earvin Johnson, talked about his persona as Magic Johnson almost being like a character he played. He was a celebrity, a star, for the Lakers in the '80s. A reporter from the documentary *Magic & Bird: A Courtship of Rivals* said, "I really do believe he looks upon Magic Johnson, as a movie character he played."

Magic himself said, "The Magic ego swallowed Earvin a little bit. But that's okay, because I couldn't win five championships without that."[63]

That's the obsessive component. Inflated ego and getting out of balance is part of the journey to greatness.

I'm somebody who speaks of conscious command, and I'm one of the people who needs it the most. I have such a low baseline that I need that IMS and alpha brain wave power to move me up the scale from zero to cocksure. If I didn't have more cocksure than some others, I'd be stuck in that low baseline of anxiety and depression.

---

63   *Magic & Bird: A Courtship of Rivals,* directed by Ezra Edelman (HBO Sports, 2010).

On the flip side, some people have too much cocksureness, and the IMS and alpha brain waves can help them check themselves to move more toward zero. Because they have a higher baseline, it is easier for them than someone like me to hang out on the cocksure extreme.

Magic Johnson probably started with a higher baseline than mine, so he was able to take his high-performance even further than me. It doesn't mean that my high performance isn't the same as his work ethic. It just means our baselines were different.

Ego is fantastic. Anyone who walks around saying "No ego" is fooling themselves. Sometimes you need to get that ego out of control because it is the only way to raise yourself from zero. We all need to think much higher of ourselves, or the IMS will find a way to shoot us down. The line between confidence and cocksure is fine, but they both tie into success. Confidence in who you are and what you're doing is what's needed to reach your goals.

Going out of control on ego isn't necessarily a bad thing for the people who take those opportunities to grow, learn, and better themselves through conscious command and the IMS. It becomes dangerous when that cocksure ego becomes self-destructive because you aren't taking those opportunities to reflect, learn, and change how you interact with people and the world.

If the IMS is trained to be reflexively positive, you can avoid those self-sabotaging loops and break free for a high-performance life.

CHAPTER 6

FALSE PEDESTALS, EGO, AND ALPHA BRAIN WAVES

Former heavyweight boxing champion Mike Tyson has a firm grip on what his ego represents. He spoke a lot about ego with Joe Rogan in a January 17, 2019, podcast. Tyson told Rogan that he doesn't work out and train anymore because it "reactivates his ego."[64]

But Tyson went viral on social media in 2020 because of a video of him training. He concluded the 20-second clip by saying, "I'm back."[65]

---

64   Joe Rogan and Mike Tyson, "The Joe Rogan Experience, Episode #1227," PowerfulJRE YouTube Channel, January 17, 2019, video, 1:27:16, https://www.youtube.com/watch?v=7MNv4_rTkfU.

65   Josh Katzowitz, "Mike Tyson Proclaims 'I'm Back,'" After Dropping Another Vicious Training Video," Forbes, May 11, 2020, https://www.forbes.com/sites/joshkatzowitz/2020/05/11/mike-tyson-proclaims-im-back-after-dropping-another-vicious-training-video/?sh=32287bfe5fa3.

Tyson is perhaps the most vicious, powerful heavyweight boxer in history. A series of misfortune and luck put him on the path at a young age. Tyson had been arrested 38 times by age 13, according to a *Rolling Stone* interview. Lorna Mae Smith-Tyson, his mother, died when Mike was only 16. His trainer, Cus D'Amato, became his legal guardian. D'Amato died three days after Tyson's 11th professional fight, leaving Mike with no guidance or adult figure in his life. Despite the hardships, Tyson became the youngest heavyweight champion ever (age 20) in 1986 when he beat Trevor Berbick.

D'Amato once told Tyson, "Your greatest asset can become your greatest weakness."[66] Tyson's ego propelled him to championship status, fame, and riches. But his ego took over his entire life and changed him from immortal gladiator to vulnerable human being. His first career loss to James "Buster" Douglas on February 11, 1990, sent shock waves around the world.

Tyson's career was interrupted when he served three years in prison from 1992–1995. He won his first four fights upon his return to the ring. But Tyson was never the same fighter. He lost twice to Evander Holyfield, including the infamous ear-biting disqualification. The Orlin Norris fight was ruled a no-contest after a late-hit foul by Tyson in the first round. His victory over Andrew Golota was later rescinded after Tyson tested positive for cannabis. The loss to Lennox Lewis meant Tyson never beat either of the two best heavyweights of his era.[67]

---

66   Brian Kenny, "Iron Mike Looks Tough as Steel," ESPN Boxing, January 15, 1999, https://assets.espn.go.com/boxing/columns/abramowitz_roberto/23669.html.

67   "Mike Tyson," *Encyclopedia Britannica*, last modified March 7, 2024, https://www. britannica.com/biography/Mike-Tyson.

How could someone at the top of his game, who'd risen through adversity and had broken records, take such a turn for the worse before reaching his true potential?

It all comes back to ego and false pedestals.

EGO-LESS TO EGO-GO

Austrian neurologist Sigmund Freud expanded on the concept of ego with his 1920s personality theories. He posited that the human psyche is made up of three parts: the id, ego, and super-ego. The id represents our primal instincts and urges, including sexual desires and hunger. It operates on the so-called pleasure principle that seeks immediate gratification. The superego is the moral arbiter. It represents ideals taught by society, family, and other influences.[68]

We can see the quandary in those old Bugs Bunny cartoons depicting a devil (id) standing on one shoulder and an angel (super-ego) on the other. Both were telling Bugs how to handle various situations. It's ultimately up to the self (ego) to determine the correct and most advantageous course.

Various practices abound on trying to control the ego. Eastern religions, for example, teach that "egolessness" is a sought-after mental state and that separation from ego is the path to enlightenment. But our egos define our true selves. A properly utilized ego amplifies purpose and guides men toward their goals. Conscious

---

68   "Know About Sigmund Freud's Triple-Decker Model of the Human Psyche: Id, Ego, and Superego," Britannica, accessed March 8, 2024, https://www.britannica.com/video/186442/human-psyche-model-ego-Sigmund-Freud-id.

command means training your brain to recognize and then maximize your innate abilities and gifts.

Men—indeed, all people—cannot run from their true selves. Mike Tyson understands that God gave him a gift that facilitated his roller-coaster ride through life. He suppressed his imbalanced ego because he could not control it. But suppressing ego is not good practice. The solution is ego-go, which means finding balance between our natural gifts and flaws. Tyson will always be a fighter. He is also a deeply spiritual sage, father, and husband who found equilibrium in his 40s. Tyson has been ego-go since 2020.

THE AUTHENTIC SELF AND ZERO-ZERO MINDSET

Michael Formica is a psychotherapist and Initiate of the Shankya Yoga lineage. His writings in *Psychology Today* articulate the negative effects of self-objectification. Placing yourself or others on pedestals, false to otherwise reality, diminishes the authentic self of both parties.[69]

The Center for Growth in Philadelphia defines the authentic self as doing what you say. It's not your career, possessions, or roles in life (father, brother, etc.). The authentic self encompasses your thoughts, words, and actions being played out in real life. Those who are not living as their authentic selves tend to self-mask their mental deficiencies by going into "people-pleasing" mode.[70]

---

69   Michael J. Formica, "Authenticity and Self-Perception," *Psychology Today*, October 7, 2008, https://www.psychologytoday.com/us/blog/enlightened-living/200810/authenticity-and-self-perception.

70   Jennifer Foust, "What It Means to Be Your Authentic Self?," The Center for Growth, accessed March 8, 2024, https://www.thecenterforgrowth.com/tips/what-it-means-to-be-your-authentic-self.

Of course, there is a time and place for the different aspects of our personality. Your authentic self may not be the best presentation for a job interview. It's imperative, however, to understand that these variations of the self are situational. Social-media presentations, for instance, are situational. Most are practiced in presenting their "best" self, not their authentic self on Facebook, Instagram, etc. But too many "likes" and "retweets" (false pedestals) can lead you down the path of losing your authentic self.

NBA forward Antoine Walker is today a humble man who experienced life's most extreme highs and frustrating lows. Walker was an all-state forward at Mount Carmel High School in Chicago. He earned a full-ride athletic scholarship to NCAA powerhouse Kentucky in 1994. Walker, at age 19, won an NCAA championship in 1996 and was selected as the sixth-overall pick in the NBA Draft that same year by the Boston Celtics. He won an NBA championship with the Miami Heat in 2006. Walker retired from the NBA in 2008, having earned over $110 million in salary. But due to extreme generosity, indulgence, and bad investment, Walker lost his fortune and filed for bankruptcy in 2010. He chronicled this chapter of his life in the 2020 documentary *Gone in an Instant*.[71]

Personal development ceases when individuals are placed on pedestals by themselves and others. Mr. Walker, like many young entrepreneurs, athletes, and actors who come upon material success early, fall victim to false pedestals. The maxim goes that "money doesn't change you; it makes you more of what you already are."

---

71   *Gone in an Instant*, directed by Anthony Holt (Mammoth Entertainment, 2020).

In the beginning of my journey with self-development, I thought that I was going to reach this stage of enlightenment where I was no longer going to be held back by my traumas. I thought meditation could get me there, and that one day, I would arrive at this "aha" stage of enlightenment that would set me free from my past. Instead, I kept finding that I was just right back in the thick of it, as if I hadn't started my self-development or had any moments of enlightenment at all.

I kept putting myself and my self-development on a false pedestal, and it just crushed me and kept me down. I became more depressed. It took me a long time to realize that there's no "having arrived." I call it the Zero-Zero Mindset. A conscious man or woman knows that the journey is everlasting from one day to the next. Every time you wake up, you have to treat it like you're back at zero again, regardless of how good the day before was or how much progress you've made. Any athletic team that plays like the score is zero-zero, whether they are up or down, will have the best opportunity to capture and sustain a lead. Same goes for enlightenment. You have to attack it like the score is zero-zero in order to sustain and move with enlightenment.

It took me a long time to arrive at that realization, and when I did, it finally set me free. That's when I had a deep intellectual and emotional understanding that if I didn't put in the work, my performance and quality of life were going to drop. My subconscious stories of lack and limitation will always be on the sidelines begging, "Put me in coach!" As soon as you falter or drop awareness, stories come in and without conscious command, it is easy to fall back into old reflexive patterns and habits.

After accepting that insight, I knew what I had to do. As long as I was here on this Earth, I had to put in the work for conscious command. Otherwise, the skills atrophy. It's atrophy of the IMS if you don't put in the work, atrophy of muscles if you don't keep training, atrophy of the nervous system, etc.

It doesn't matter how great of a job you've done to this point with self-development and physical training, or digital deprivation and story trapping (which will be discussed in the next chapter). If you don't keep up with it, it slips away. It's all gone, and the subconscious has taken over.

So, I kept thinking I could arrive at a certain level of success or enlightenment, and I would be fine. It made me realize that no matter what level of success I reached in this life, I'm always going to have to put in the work as if I don't see success or gain emotional balance. That's how I have to attack it. I have to be real with myself and my trauma.

WHAT FALSE PEDESTALS ARE YOU ON?

I have learned that I have to reject false pedestals, which aren't just expectations we put on ourselves. Sometimes, those expectations come from an external source.

One time when I was at a café working on the content for this book, a gentleman came up to me and asked what I was working on. I told him what I was up to, and we got to talking about the subject matter. He went into talking about this program he was following where you're supposed to do all these weekly tasks. It was a self-training, self-leadership program, much like what we have at Prodigy Mindset.

One of the tasks was stepping out of your comfort zone by breaking out and engaging in a way you don't normally. That's exactly what he was doing there with me. He was a good-looking guy, young, looked like an athlete, cut from the same cloth as me.

No one would look at him and think he lacked confidence in a social setting. This guy in the café is standing there telling me these things. He tells me, "People look at me a lot and talk to me like I have it together and I'm confident. But I don't really feel like I have any of this in me to the degree people would expect."

Other people in his life put him up on a false pedestal of confidence and this social persona, but he didn't feel that way, so he was there working to meet their expectations. So many times, I've worked with men just like him. I was one of them once.

I've had people in the program who watch my videos and tell me, "Man, you make talking and recording videos look so easy." But what they don't see in the background is that every time I get ready to do a video, I'm thinking to myself, "Ugh, I don't want to do a video." For me, it never gets easier. I've done hundreds of videos and I've done all the mindset work, but I still need to consciously give myself that confidence in order to make my videos. I have to prep in alpha before I move into beta.

I make it look easy to the casual observer because I do a lot of work toward empowering myself prior to the moment. I "make it look easy" or appear good at it because I put in the work.

Similarly, my youngest daughter wants to be a gymnast. She trains hard, but sometimes she finds herself defeated by her own thoughts before she gets to practice. I tell her that to achieve her gymnast goals, it's going to hurt, it's going to be hard work, and she's going to struggle. Self-sabotaging thoughts could easily be the result, but if she always remembers to prepare herself mentally before walking through those gym doors, she'll see huge changes in herself and great results.

My own struggle with videos as well as the struggles of the man in the café were less physical than my daughter's struggle, but we still had to do the same amount of mental stretching, warm-up, and preparation that a gymnast does before a competition.

Since I'm leading the programs at Prodigy Mindset, the site that holds all my programs and future content, participants will think I have all the answers, quick easy fixes, and ask me questions before they start like, "Do I need to quit drinking or smoking?" or "So, I'm about to go on a diet to lose weight. Is it a good idea?" That's too cocksure for me to say as a coach. I can't pretend to have all the answers for an individual training in conscious command, but I can help them get in the state to know the answers for themselves.

I say, "I don't know, but you'll find out." It is all about the individual's experience and connecting with their authentic self away from false pedestals. For me, it's not about telling people what to do but helping them get in that creative space and that place of empowerment where they know what they should do and go after it. The only secret is to know your true self. Otherwise, you're faking it.

When I first moved back to Southern California, I had a cocksure roommate that challenged my image of myself. He would always say things like, "It's a good thing you're good looking."

Maybe his quip seems like a compliment or a positive, but to me, it made me question a lot about who I was, my capabilities, and how other people saw me.

When you think about it, if someone is thinking that about me, and they are saying it in this sarcastic way, then they seem to like me, hate me, and have jealousy toward me about this thing (my looks), and it just becomes who you are to them.

But what does it matter if I'm good looking? Does that define my authentic self?

Statements like that come off as a compliment but are really more of a veiled insult, like saying, "You're lucky you have looks because you have nothing else going for you."

The guy who walked up to me in the café wasn't as confident in the areas that everyone expected him to be confident in. He had to work on that. It doesn't matter if he was good looking or appeared confident because he couldn't utilize those attributes in the way for which other people are jealous of him.

There are people who think we have it all together because of our "look," but we don't. Even someone like me who had the athletics and looks and the acting career. As an actor, there's a certain amount of physical attraction that helps pave the way for certain parts. Sometimes, while I was acting, I'd think back to those comments my roommate made and wonder if I had the right talent or if it was all based on my looks. It was a false pedestal I stood on based on the perceptions of others. So, I was still fucking myself up in my head, and a lot of times, it was coming from the things that people think are positives like "looks."

It's the weight of what people think of us and the expectations people have for us. Magic Johnson's sister said she thought that her brother Earvin had to live up to the name "Magic." It was a persona that people had expectations for. A lot of pro athletes, celebrities, and public figures have these characters they play based on what's expected of them, and when they fall short, it is all over the media and they are judged by the court of public opinion.[72]

But we put them all on false pedestals rather than acknowledging that they are human, they have traumas, and they aren't always as together as they appear on the outside.

That element there, I find fascinating, because I work with people who you'd think are very confident, but under it all, there's self-doubt and self-sabotaging behavior. Like them and because of what others thought of me, I ended up on these slippery slopes where I thought, "Oh, well I've got this going for me, so I can or should do this." But when I slipped off that pedestal and couldn't meet others' expectations, I couldn't figure out what was wrong with me.

---

72   *Magic & Bird.*

When you're in that alpha state you're able to elevate those thoughts and situations on a higher level of critical thinking. For me, I realized that if I'm "really, really, really ridiculously good looking" like Derek Zoolander, some people aren't going to like me for it. It is what it is.

FALSE PEDESTALS AND THE ALPHA BRAIN WAVES

People put us on pedestals, and we feel the weight of their expectations. The only way to navigate the effect of their judgment and to keep it from bringing us down is to know who we are. It all ties back into the IMS…we are who we tell ourselves we are.

Just like consistent repetitions in the gym yield stronger muscles, the brain needs those same constant IMS repetitions to maximize potential.

A positively charged and reflexive IMS is going to get you through the expectations of others. That guy who came up to me in the café needed to live up to that confidence expectation that others had of him. He was holding himself accountable and doing self-study, which is self-leadership.

The stuff that's floating around on the internet and pop-culture ideals of the alpha males—it doesn't matter what's out there or what expectations there are—they all are false pedestals. With conscious command and the alpha brain waves, it is possible to connect with your authentic self and be who you tell yourself you are rather than be who everyone sees you as.

Mike Tyson clearly lost his edge while he was still boxing in his youth. It was downhill from there. Same with Rowdy Ronda Rousey. She stopped being rowdy in the UFC. Conor McGregor hasn't been so notorious in the ring since his leg injury. It took him nearly three years to ramp himself back up and announce his return to the ring. Is that too cocksure for me to say? Their egos and IMS were inflated when they were on top. And sometimes that's what it takes. But it can get messy if we get inflated through unconscious momentum. A single life event can shake you to the core, and it can rip away the momentum.

If you get your greatness unconsciously, that is a pedestal that's going to get pulled out from under you. You've got to do it in a conscious way.

Unlike Tyson, George Foreman suffered a major career setback. After suffering severe heatstroke and extreme fatigue, Foreman had a near-death experience that gave him a new, spiritual perspective on life and took him out of the ring. But he overcame it by finding his way to the alpha brain waves. In the movie chronicling Foreman's career, his trainer is yelling at him to, "Let him out," referring to the old, angry Foreman from before.

George said, "I'm going to do it my way." He found that balance to be a fighter while also maintaining his spiritual convictions. And at age 45, he came back in that alpha mindset, not relying on anger as his driver, and dominated as a fighter by doing it the alpha way. George Foreman was able to come back by doing it his way. He said it was because he found Jesus, that he was no longer the angry George. It was his source for conscious command and discovering the alpha mindset. Prayer, meditation, IMS repetition, it's all the same. It's all part of that alpha frequency and its manifestation processes.[73]

Mike Tyson described training as reactivating his ego because he didn't have that conscious command over his ego.[74] He wasn't set up to see that it was the IMS that kept him going while the rest of his metaphorical fuel tank was empty. As a result, some other story was able to slip in. He was unconscious to it, and his entire image of himself and his career unraveled.

We get locked into false pedestals of success and materialism, and it takes us away from the work it took to get there. If you become unconscious of the alpha mindset and stop consciously prepping in alpha before beta situations and events, even if it isn't in a literal boxing ring, you can get lost in that false pedestal persona and lose your authentic self.

THE STARTER-BLOCK MINDSET

It's not what time you wake up, it's how you wake up.

One important pedestal I had to overcome was thinking I needed to wake up at 4, 5, or 6 a.m. to produce at a high-performance level. As if that window of time determines everything. Your alpha brain activity commences immediately when you wake up in the morning. Scientists describe it as a state of

---

73 *Big George Foreman*, directed by George Tillman Jr. (2023, Culver City, CA: Affirm Films, and Los Angeles: Mandalay Pictures).

74 Joe Rogan and Mike Tyson, "Being Hypnotized to Win," JRE Clips YouTube Channel, January 17, 2019, video, 5:12, https://www.youtube.com/watch?app=desktop&v=ibCdGpG3GTU.

wakeful rest. It's the ideal state of consciousness for learning and solving complex tasks.[75]

I found that I could wake with the alpha mindset at any time of day or night once I put the focus on winning my very first thought with conscious command. That knowledge was much better than trying to live by someone else's schedule. Time of day was a false pedestal for me because I kept asking myself, "What the fuck is wrong with me? I can't wake up and get it done at five in the morning like some of these thought leaders do." I realized that I was alive at night. So, instead of going to sleep and waking up at odd hours and feeling bad about it, I was busy riding that alpha frequency. I made waking up reflexive with conscious command and IMS repetition. My sluggish and tanked-feeling mornings as a child were no longer an excuse. I could consciously choose IMS repetition and create the runner's high for myself. I could choose to do something about how I woke up, no matter what time it was. That practice was a game changer. I call it the Starter-Block Mindset.

My sleep patterns change based on the season and my work schedule, but there are times where I go to bed right after the sun rises and wake up right at sunset. I sleep during the day, but I see the sunrise, and sometimes I'll sit there through the process and meditate. I get to consciously move from beta to alpha and reflect on all the work I was able to accomplish through the night. Then, I go to bed an hour after sunrise. I still catch the end of the day when the sun sets. I come alive at sunset.

---

75   Jay Summer, "Alpha Waves and Sleep," SleepFoundation.org, last modified December 22, 2023, https://www.sleepfoundation.org/how-sleep-works/alpha-waves-and-sleep.

It works great for my personality, and I get just as much done as anyone else.

I've heard people say, "Make your bed, every morning, if you do, it's going to change your life." But the process of waking to consciousness is where the change happens. If you start by making the bed, I don't know how many thoughts could go through your mind between waking and actually getting to the action of making the bed.

Every thought leader stresses the importance of a good morning routine. Commonly suggested rituals are hydrating, stretching, meditation, journaling, and making the bed first thing in the morning. Although beneficial, these morning practices are challenging in the digital age. If the sound of prompting apps does not arouse us, most of us wake up to our phone's alarm. Unconsciously reacting to thoughts of needing to read a text, email, or headline first thing in the morning is a slippery slope. That time is where limiting thoughts and self-talk can exist immediately. Meditation, journaling, and other morning practices get crushed. Waking unconsciously brings up past stories, subconscious stories of the day before, or the month before, or the year before, which leads to falling into some unconscious pattern.

How well we wake to conscious command and leave our starter blocks is just as important and nuanced. A prime example is found in sprinters. They have two choices: focus on the motor or sensory set while anticipating the sound of the gun. It is favorable for one to focus on the motor set, the actual movement off the block. A slower time result may occur if a runner chooses to focus on the sensory set in anticipation of the gun. The brain has to acknowledge the gun before the body responds. Instead, concentrating on the explosive power from your lead arm and leg is recommended. The technique can lead to a .10-second gain.[76]

For those of us in the everyday world, the idea is to put our focus on conscious command immediately upon waking, "win" our first thoughts, and achieve the alpha brain wave frequency.

LEVELING THE PLAYING FIELD

Although it isn't in the Bible, there's an adage that goes, "God helps those who help themselves." The IMS is that self-help. I've been on both sides of the coin when it comes to false pedestals and trying to work my way back from a life-shaking event.

For example, when I was living in L.A. at 33, I played soccer in an adult league. My playing style was with speed and using my body to push people around. But I wasn't taking care of myself for my playing style and effort. I wasn't warming up or stretching properly. One day, my hamstrings just failed, and it was a rough, traumatic injury.

It became a three- four-year problem I worked on, and in that time, I wasn't playing soccer. After a while, I'd unconsciously turn, pivot, and run up the stairs, and in that process my hamstrings would tweak again for a couple of weeks.

I was so depressed with that injury. I gained weight, and I wasn't working out. I very much know what it is like to go through an

---

76 Tyler Read, "Explosive Workouts for Speed, Power, and Strength," Healthline, April 18, 2022, https://www.healthline.com/health/fitness/explosive-workouts.

injury as one who goes through life unconsciously. I got sucked into the ego and depression that I couldn't play soccer. I never played again in any leagues. It was sad, painful…it was a lot of things. I could have done better at handling it. And like many other athletes who suffered injuries, I was too wrapped up in my wounded ego to come back from it.

There are a lot of cocksure athletes who reached greatness unconsciously and think, "This setback would never happen to me." Then it does, and they don't have the reflexive IMS to sustain conscious command over the injury and get their fire back. That's what I see when athletes lose their edge and exhibit a noticeable decline or can't recover from a large life event.

Now, my recent neck injury and recovery is on the other end. I provided the example of being injured and needing to come back at the end of the season without any fear. I put in the conscious work to ensure that my IMS remained positively reflexive, and it enabled my speedy recovery.

When I got injured recently, my own ego went in the direction of saying, "I can't be that guy, that influencer on social media, that go injured." I don't see a lot of the influencers I follow getting hurt, at least not ones that are posting about it. I kept asking myself, "What did I do wrong?" I had to check my own ego and own that a setback was happening for me. Through it, I've helped a lot of people who have suffered injuries.

In another instance, I was working out from a place of anger instead of alpha one night, and I noticed my shoulder looked strange.

It didn't look dislocated, it just looked odd. I was so emotionally messy that night. It didn't hurt at the time, and I went home and went to bed. I woke up the next morning to what felt like a five-alarm fire. It was like I had gotten into a fight or a wreck, and it just blew up. I was in a lot of pain. My vagus nerve was all caught up and out of whack, holding the trauma.

For a good grip of days, these injuries tested my mettle against physical and emotional pain. Trying to see that it was happening for me and not against me was difficult.

When I came out the other side, I was emotionally and spiritually exhausted. That zero-zero mentality got me back to baseline. I was reminded that every day, the score is zero-zero and the work has to be put in for times like those.

The Zero-Zero Mindset is understanding that we are evolving and that every single day we are here is another chance to participate in it. The world is going to keep moving.

If I let my bruised ego get in the way, I wouldn't have been able to continue to have that "search and destroy" attitude through the whole injury process and see that it was an opportunity to help other people. Through my IMS and reflexivity, I didn't let my ego get in the way. I wasn't stuck on being the guy who failed. It is hard to say things are happening for you if you are not in conscious command because you can't see the opportunities, the synchronicity of time and spiritual numbers, the little things that represent bigger things. Those are all the things that help us feel connected to a greater path and purpose.

Think of enlightenment like our seasons, constantly changing and shifting. When you train in conscious awareness and conscious command, you set yourself up to win because when that season changes again, you're prepared.

That process is very delicate. With my depression from my soccer injury, I didn't take care of myself and heal properly. Not only do I see it happen in other athletes or people at critical stages in their lives, but I've experienced both sides.

It is important not to think you've arrived anywhere. It's transient. Your subconscious stories will be ready to jump back in the game, but you've got to level the playing field. The history of that saying goes back to how two teams would switch sides at half-time because there was a slope in the field, and they didn't want one team to have an unfair advantage.

You're always sloped down into the subconscious, so if you think about it that way, you've got to level your own playing field with the Zero-Zero Mindset while ramping yourself up with your IMS.

CHAPTER 7

THE TRIFECTA OF CONSCIOUS COMMAND—A.K.A., CONSCIOUS CREATIVITY

Creativity is not a talent. It is not a talent, it is a way of operating.

— John Cleese

There are three main components to elevating conscious command—a.k.a., conscious creativity. Together, they create a synergy that allows conscious awareness and opens the mind for conscious command and the IMS. The trifecta includes digital deprivation: first, abstaining from all non-work-related digital media; second, fasting: adhering to an eating schedule based on a 16/8-hour timeframe, 20/4-hour timeframe, and a 24-hour timeframe, known as the "eat-stop-eat" method. The third is story trapping: consciously identifying, trapping, and fueling past outmoded subconscious stories of lack and limitation. With conscious command, we trap and pivot into purpose-driven action.

Few people know how to do it, and fewer are willing to put in the effort to learn. When I was a personal trainer, I was really bothered by client turnover. These people were successful—judges, lawyers, doctors. They'd reached a level of purpose in their lives and career. Yes, they were successful, but they were also practiced in denying themselves proper self-care, which is why they wouldn't stick with the training. Without a focus on conscious awareness, a new endeavor like training with me at the gym on top of their current day-to-day life was too much to ask.

They were so well practiced in being distracted by intrusive thoughts, worrying about what other people at the gym thought of them, how they looked doing something, etc. As a personal trainer (and in my own development), I was ready to teach, and their distractions frustrated me. The problem was that they weren't ready to learn. They hadn't done anything to allow themselves to be in a conscious state where their commitment could thrive. Conscious awareness and conscious creativity were the bottom line, and when I understood it, I directed my pursuits entirely to that lane. Training for conscious command would become my study, practice, and service.

That understanding and observation made me realize early on when I was creating my program that if I was going to get people to really change and feel what the work does for them, then I'm going to have to get them to create space for that. I'm going to have to get their conscious command way up.

Right away, digital deprivation popped into my mind. The answer was right there. It's what I'd do for everyone working with me. I knew it would help them be more aware of what we were doing.

After that, I'd tell them we're going to do some fasting—fasting for conscious awareness. Fasting and reaching the point where you are empty and being hungry gives you the opportunity to turn into self, become aware of the body, be primal, and come into alpha. We all have the innate quality to reach an alpha state and turn inward to become self-aware. Tools like fasting allow you to access that suppressed primal mindset.

When I bring that aspect into the fold with a client, I let them know, yeah, you're going to get hungry, but it is a purposeful pivot point for self-awareness. We're using it as a tool. Getting into that state is supplied by digital deprivation because you start to see your impulses toward the digital world. Those impulses are a type of unconscious story. Once you're aware of that story, you can think about how you are going to write a new one. When you have the awareness, you can stop reaching for your phone and pivot, writing yourself a new story. Practicing the process makes it reflexive.

> *Shakespeare, Leonardo da Vinci, Benjamin Franklin,*
> *and Abraham Lincoln never saw a movie, heard a*
> *radio, or looked at a television…They had loneliness*
> *and knew what to do with it. They were not afraid*
> *of being lonely because they knew that was when the*
> *creative mood in them would work.*
>
> — **Carl Sandburg**

DIGITAL DEPRIVATION

I believe that 10 days of digital deprivation is the necessary amount of time to really benefit from that separation. It can take as little as one day to feel mental clarity when abstaining from digital media. I choose 10 days as a goal because it is realistic and enough time for us to fully understand the benefits. I do it in line with the cycles of the moon every month to ensure conscious command.

Digital deprivation is going to look a little different for everyone. Some people have jobs that require them to use computers or phones. Other people have kids, and they need to keep an open line of communication through a cell phone. When I talk about digital deprivation, I mean abstaining from digital media outside your core responsibilities. Don't sit down and watch TV at the end of the day. If you're driving somewhere, turn off the radio and podcasts and drive in silence. It is drawing the line between what you need to do and what you can let go of.

Digital deprivation pulls the noise out. You start getting silent with yourself, start to hear your voice, catch your thoughts, and thinking. Then you start trapping and pivoting. When there's no digital noise, you can hear your thinking and internal dialogue clearly. That approach is how to first tap into the IMS.

Digital deprivation kicks off on the first day of our training programs.

You have to train for conscious awareness. We all were brought into this digital world. Some of us once existed in a less digital world, but most of us have been in this digital age from birth or our youngest years. Did anyone actually have a strategy for adapting to that transition? Did anyone say, "Yes, this is a pivotal change in time, so make sure you don't unconsciously adapt to it." That adaptation might have looked messy for some of us, and it might have snowballed out of control.

How many people unconsciously adapted to the digital world? I'll tell you: everyone. Before we knew it, we were in it. To keep self-sabotaging behavior at bay and find balance within the zero-to-cocksure scale, the IMS needs to be trained in a strategy to navigate the digital world.

If you're just doing digital things all the time, never taking breaks, going on vacations just to do more digital things, you're not thinking as well as you could be. You're just not. Between the overstimulation and the absolute garbage out there on media, it diminishes your conscious awareness.

Sometimes, during digital deprivation, people will unconsciously reach for the television remote but then think, "Oh, I screwed up. I almost turned on the TV." It isn't screwing up to me. "No, you caught yourself. Even if it was two minutes in, you became aware, and you pivoted."

Beautiful, you got it! You're now getting into that conscious awareness state of mind.

Take such opportunities of self-awareness, habitual impulses, and conscious awareness. Once those realizations arise, that's where story trapping comes in. That moment can be a part of a bigger story that always wants to beat yourself down even if it's done in humor. It's about seeing moments like them for what they are and trapping them. No story is too small to trap. Honor the details, and the details will honor you.

The first 10 days with digital deprivation is reaching conscious command and a higher level of thinking. By day five, the affirmation from chapter 4 comes in because you're conscious enough to start working with the IMS. Digital deprivation is the first of the three major components of training the IMS and reaching the alpha state.

FASTING

The goal of fasting is inner unity.

— **Thomas Merton, quoting Confucius,**
The Way of Chuang-Tzu

Fasting, for me, is about conscious command. While there are many other reported benefits of fasting like anti-aging, reversing Type 2 diabetes, and weight loss, I see them as by-products of fasting. The true benefit is conscious command.[77]

The 20/4-hour timetable with 20 hours of fasting and a four-hour window for eating is the schedule on which I function the best. There's a third option, the eat-stop-eat method where you eat one meal every 24 hours. I'll do that when I'm looking to make some quick advances, but I primarily stick to the 20/4 fasting plan. So, the individual has choices on a preferred fasting window, but each method leads to conscious awareness.

---

77   "To Fast or Not to Fast," NIH News in Health, November 2019, https://newsin-health.nih.gov/2019/12/fast-or-not-fast.

Personally, I don't think anyone needs to eat outside of an eight-hour window. Packing in three meals just doesn't make sense to me. We've seen, through fossil evidence, how people lived and evolved. Our ancestors weren't eating three meals a day. Hunting and gathering consumed the majority of daily activity, eating when the opportunity arose, often fasting for large portions of the day. Neither was food stored in the quantities that we store them now. In that environment, you couldn't store a carcass in the back of the shelter because some predator or scavenger would ransack the place. Food might have seemed scarce, but early humans were a lot more consciously aware of their environment and their needs. Today, we've packed all this eating in with long-term food storage, three meals a day, restaurants with large portions, and fast food in our lives. I think it's just absolute chaos.

If you're eating three times a day, there's more of a chance to unconsciously eat something bad for your health, and worse, not even remember that the thing hurts your stomach or messes with your digestion. Not only might you not remember how it will put your body in a bad state, but the mere act also opens the door for self-sabotaging thoughts and dialogue to start coming in.

Is that high performance? No. But when you have a shortened eating window, you're more aware of your body for longer periods of time and more conscious of what you're putting in your body during your eating window.

Once you've removed digital things for better clarity and you're fasting for conscious awareness, your story—that is, what is limiting you—is going to be really easy to spot.

Until you make the unconscious conscious, it will direct your life and you will call it fate.

— Attributed to C. G. Jung

STORY TRAPPING

We all tell ourselves stories in our subconscious minds. It's that little voice in your head telling you not to wear that one shirt because people think it looks weird. Or how we can talk ourselves out of something because we're worried what other people think. Most of the time, such stories aren't true, but we still get stuck in them and sometimes miss out on incredible opportunities because of them. The effect is similar to how I once talked myself out of pursuing a great passion of mine.

In chapter 1, I related how I gave up boudoir and erotic photography because I felt like I wouldn't be taken seriously as a mindset coach. I was looking at people like Tony Robbins, and no one at that level was taking nude photos of women. It was a conscious story I told myself, and it led me to giving up something I was really purposeful about.

Years later, I realized that I shouldn't sacrifice something I love, something that's a part of me, because I had told myself other people wouldn't respect me for it. At the end of the day, I wanted to be true to my authentic self, and I returned to that type of photography. My return to it was an amazing decision because the gratitude I get from the women I work with—the women who come to me for private photos to help with their own empowerment—far outweighs the fictional story I had been telling myself.

Likewise, becoming aware of your story is how you can start story trapping and rewriting your own reality. Story trapping became dominant in my own life because of my trauma. I asked myself, "Can the trauma be removed? Can I arrive at a place where it doesn't exist?" Once I really felt like the idea wasn't to "get over" my trauma but to write new reflexive subconscious stories, the result allowed me to say, "Okay, let's stop 'working' on my trauma and let's start trapping it." I didn't want it to limit me anymore.

Another example of my own story-trapping process came when I was under the impression that smoking cannabis is limiting when it comes to big fitness goals. Cannabis makes you hungry and unable to control the "munchies" or sustain boundaries, but that just isn't true for someone with conscious command. Smoking cannabis doesn't make you an unconscious or conscious being. The effect is always up to the individual and the level of conscious command achieved. I didn't think I could be high performance with cannabis because that's what I bought into. It limited me, but I became greater once I conquered that story and those impulses. I was then too conscious and too aware to act on those untrue ideas.

So, lately I fast for 20 hours, and I have a four-hour eating window. And I might burn a little cannabis throughout the day with coffee and water during my fast. To me, that's a beautiful life. I found control and peace from eating for conscious awareness while learning to trap a limiting story, but it took a long time for me to not feel guilty about my choice because I was believing in the collective's story.

Story trapping goes back to adversity and the need for not falling back into unconsciousness. Things were sometimes tragic on my road to personal development. In my early 20s, I lost my sister and my father within days of each other in two completely unrelated accidents. My father's health was failing, and I thought to myself that it might be better if he didn't have to suffer what was to come. A few days later, we were talking face to face. He took a step back and tripped over a carpet. His head hit the linoleum floor with a sound that rattled around the house, and I saw the life leave him. That same week, my sister was misprescribed medication and went into cardiac arrest. Those two losses so close together sent me spiraling. Especially with the guilt I felt over my father. I couldn't help but think I somehow manifested the accident.

I was doing these hard 180s all the time, never fully able to turn my ship around and focus on personal development. I was manic and went through a lot of self-sabotaging thoughts and behaviors. It felt bipolar because I came from a mucked-up frequency of existence and then started experiencing Zen. But in the moments between meditation, I was back to being manic again. It was almost worse than when I first started my journey in self-development because I was flipping from manic to Zen all the time.

I was all over the place…that manic state and the need to control it. I needed to gain some kind of conscious command. One time I stood in one place, and I told myself that I wasn't moving until I knew that my thoughts were my thoughts, that I wasn't going to let anything slip. I stood like that for what seemed like hours sometimes. It was like being in the moment in a deer blind.

Story trapping is like hunting. You've got to get primal. I use the hunting analogy in the program, and I get some interesting responses. One came from a national champion baseball pitcher, and he said, "Damn, it gets you into this primal sense of your conscious awareness." That's story trapping at its finest. You're hunting your unconscious thoughts like you would hunt an animal.

Hunting animals in the city is too noisy. That's why I left L.A. I needed to get a little bit more into a lower frequency. I chose to go back to Texas, and the change helped me get into that primal state. The idea of getting into the forest and hunting an animal—that's where digital deprivation comes in.

When you remove all the digital noise and stimuli, it's like you're in the forest. You can move into that frequency and hunt your own thoughts. You need the break in order to trap those moments. It might be the fasting or the digital deprivation that gives you that big revelation. That feeling of, "What have I been doing all this time? I've been in quicksand. I've been trying to do everything at a badass level in quicksand, and it's because of my limiting stories."

Story trapping is a unique point in the trifecta because every time I run ALPHA or ALPHA PRO, it's like watching a movie a second time. If it's good the first time around, the second time you notice even more about the plot—little nuggets of details—and it gets even better. You pick up on different things in the story.

It's a major player in my "aha" moments. I'm always so thankful when those moments happen. What it boils down to is conscious awareness. Before discipline comes conscious awareness. And both also comes before story trapping. I have to have the awareness to say, "Am I thinking? Am I here?" to move from beta to alpha and back again.

Those moments come to me now unconsciously, reflexively, but it will be in the story-trapping process where it begins. I've taught myself to be in conscious command before any of my events, like a meeting, presenting a contest, etc. Conscious command is operating in creativity.

BOUNDARIES AND STORY TRAPPING

I get a good amount of feedback from people who, once they start story trapping, start realizing that they may need to hang out less with certain people. That realization comes from having a shared story, and that shared story is based on feeling like you're up against adversity. We all can share that kind of stuff, but there are people who obviously have a lot of practice just talking about it and not trapping, pivoting, and fueling forward. Time to spend less time with them.

From the start, story trapping is dealing with an internal story head on, and it can be challenging. It can also be challenging to deal with the stories that you hear coming from those around you. Those stories also need to be trapped so that you can pivot and fuel forward, just like the collective story I bought into about cannabis.

Be prepared to adjust who it is that you hang out with and what you do during development. Your first inclination is thinking, "I shouldn't be hanging out with [________] or spending my time doing [_______].” With the trifecta process, you can clearly see what needs to be done. And you find that you become much more productive. It's the story trapping part of the trifecta process that allows you to realize where to set boundaries for yourself. Upon reaching that state, ALPHA and ALPHA PRO participants have been like, “Oh shit, I'm really selling myself short and not setting myself up to win by hanging out with people who aren't of the frequency that I am trying to reach. I can see the story now.”

CREATIVITY IS A FORM OF OPERATING IN THE ALPHA STATE

John Cleese, a well-known actor, author, and member of the Monty Python crew, brilliantly wrote in his book *Creativity: A Short and Cheerful Guide*: “[Creativity] is not a talent, it is a way of operating.”[78] Understanding that perspective means anyone can be creative. You just need to put yourself in that alpha state.

At the beginning of the program, you're using the synergy of this trifecta to enter the alpha state, which is the creative state. The goal at the start of the program is to get into this state, achieving conscious command and smoothly pivoting into creativity. Once you start to spot and trap your story, you start to go, “Oh, I could be doing this instead,” That's operating in creativity.

Early on I set out to figure out the baseline of self-evolution. For a very long time I've been trying to figure out that very thing, and

---

78 John Cleese, *Creativity: A Short and Cheerful Guide* (New York: Crown Publishing, 2020).

that's why I'm always talking about Mike Tyson and his discipline ideas. Because he says, and he's not the only one, it's "Discipline, discipline, discipline." But that's not where it starts. It's conscious awareness, conscious awareness, conscious awareness.

I kept thinking, "What is the baseline of conscious awareness, what creates consciousness?"

I was already at the point where I was realizing that I (and therefore you) may never get to the bottom of a trauma or PTSD. But when you're in the alpha state, you start rewriting your story and start to create new neural pathways, which allow you to become reflexive toward all those issues. Overcoming trauma becomes a by-product of the IMS and reflexivity.

That's what I love about this work. It brings all kinds of spider-webbing effects. Fasting is the same. With fasting, I'm not going for the accuracy of the perfect physique. I'm going for conscious command…the physique is a potential by-product.

With conscious command, the rest of your life can transform as well.

TAKE COMMAND IN 21 DAYS OF ALPHA

Sometimes, I get clients who want to tell me all about their problems. I politely tell them that I don't want to hear anything. If they are at a point where the trauma is too recent, too new, and they need to talk about it, that's where a therapist or psychiatrist can come in.

If I become the sounding board, I'm just enabling that story. That's not what I'm about. I'm the guy you come to when you're sick of your own unconscious bullshit…when you want to get conscious to it, and you want to create something new.

For those who are ready to move forward, digital deprivation, fasting, and story trapping takes command of conscious awareness.

While digital deprivation is only the first 10 days of the 21-day program, those who stick to digital deprivation for the entire 21-day cycle have a way better ride. Some have said, "I don't want to go back to digital media." They recognize that they'll drop conscious command all of a sudden and become caught up in some crap story.

In fact, people who stick with the trifecta for the entire program notice all kinds of changes, like with procrastination. I've had a lot of clients tell me, "The IMS gets rid of procrastination." By using the three strategies, you become aware of the procrastination, both conscious and unconscious. That awareness allows you to pivot and use your reflexive IMS to hold yourself accountable and do what you need to do.

I admit that sometimes I will take a month off from the program, but I still try to get in some days of digital deprivation. It helps me know whether I own it, or it owns me. I think that in this world, that self-check-in process should be a no brainer for all of us. Digital deprivation is the process of checking in with myself. I need to dial out in order to dial in.

FINDING YOUR WINDOW

Every program at Prodigy Mindset begins on a new or full moon. I like the new moons because they are associated with new intentions, and you get to ride into that new intention as you begin. You can set the program up with the moon and give yourself the astrological positioning that resonates with you and your current frequency.

Early on, I used to think about how cool it would be to have something like a professional sport or movie career to hold me accountable for being in great shape. I was especially drawn to action films for that reason. It's been a good 15 years since I read the fitness-related article about actors, but I believe it was Jason Statham who said that he stays 6–8 weeks out from being "movie ready."

When I read that, I thought, "That's his window! And he knows it. He knows himself that well, and he can pull it off on command." Then, I asked myself, "Do I know my window?" Shit, no, I didn't. And realizing it only added to my limiting stories and belief that I could ever be an actor like Statham. I can tell you that the doubt persisted as long as I related only to the disciplines of physical training and dieting to Statham's level of fitness and awareness.

For many years during that time, I yo-yoed in and out of great shape. Sometimes, it took a full year to come back from over-shooting my window. It wasn't until I pulled my focus away from the physical training and dieting and put the spotlight on training for conscious command that I was able to keep to my window. I found my window for conscious command the way Statham knew his window for being "movie ready." To be clear, when I found my anchor in the moon, I found my window. If I start my 21-day training period on the first day of a new moon, I finish on the 21st day of that same month. And I won't pick my training for conscious command back up until the next new moon.

That gives me about 10 days to get lax on training for conscious command. But I know that a 10-day window can get out of hand. I know that window can turn into months if I'm not careful. And I know that someone like myself, a self-sabotager, doesn't really need any more than 10 days of being lax on conscious command. Just like Statham aims to stay within that 6–8-week "movie ready" window for the purpose of physical ability and overall aesthetics on screen, my goal is to always try to stay within that 10-day window for conscious command. And more often than not, I find myself looking "movie ready" as a result.

Aligning the program with the moon cycles, that 21-day period, I went to work on conscious awareness so that I could give myself a better opportunity, a better life. And that's exactly what turning to the cosmos with the IMS helped me accomplish.

CHAPTER 8

THE IMS AND THE COSMOS

I really wouldn't know anything about consistency if it weren't for the cosmos.

Men have observed the stars for more than 30,000 years. In fact, star maps existed long before maps of the Earth. The ancient Sumerians are generally credited with first mapping the constellations and planetary movements. Ancient Egyptians predicted floods, famine, and other events based on planetary alignment. Archaeologists unearthed what many believe to be the first astrologer's board, discovered in 2012 in Croatia. The artifact dates back two millennia and features engraved images of Cancer, Gemini, and Pisces astrological signs.

One of the least talked about astrological breakthroughs in history demonstrated both the power of the cosmos and ingenuity of men.[79] Divers discovered the Antikythera Mechanism in 1901 off the Greek island with the same name. According to the Smithsonian, the object was aboard a merchant ship that sank sometime in the first century BCE. The 2,000-year-old handheld "astronomical calculator" helped the Greeks predict eclipses and other astronomical events. Researchers refer to it as the "first analog computer" due to its relative sophistication. This device is still being studied, and I suspect what science understands and accepts about it will change over time.[80]

Scientists are still trying to figure out what exactly the device does since all that was found were 82 corroded, rusty fragments, which constitute about one-third of the original mechanism. But researchers at the University College London announced that they are creating a theoretical model of the machine.[81]

Dr. Tony Freeth, the lead researcher on the project, said in a statement that his team's model is the first to incorporate all the physical and written evidence as to the device's structure and function. Two important pieces of data were derived from X-rays of the front cover. It highlights the numbers 462 and 442. The former refers to the synodic period of Venus; the latter is the synodic period of Saturn. Antikythera Research Team member Dr. David Higgon said the team matched evidence of

79   "Did You Know? The Influence of Astrology in the Science of Astronomy Along the Silk Roads," UNESCO, accessed March 8, 2024, https://en.unesco.org/silkroad/content/did-you-know-influence-astrology-science-astronomy-along-silk-roads.

80   Tony Freeth, "An Ancient Greek Astronomical Calculation Machine Reveals New Secrets," *SciAm*, January 1, 2022, https://www.scientificamerican.com/article/an-ancient-greek-astronomical-calculation-machine-reveals-new-secrets/.

81   "Experts Recreate a Mechanical Cosmos for the World's First Computer," UCL News, March 12, 2021, https://www.ucl.ac.uk/news/2021/mar/experts-recreate-mechanical-cosmos-worlds-first-computer.

two fragments and found the exact 462-year planetary period related for Venus.

Researchers are still trying to replicate the machine as closely as possible to the original mechanism. Thus, they are using no lathes or other technology not available then, although I do believe some researchers have branched out and are using more updated technology to try and recreate the missing pieces.

Indeed, all throughout human history, we have evidence of the importance of the stars, zodiac, celestial bodies, and the cosmos. Watching the skies was a cultural part of the development of many human civilizations, along with what gave rise to certain disciplines. There's even new evidence to suggest that complex mathematics were in use by astronomers centuries before emerging formally in central Europe.[82]

The Declaration of Independence, the precursor of modern democracy, was signed on a special eclipse. Known to practice astrology, Benjamin Franklin chose July 4, 1776, the day of a five-planet planetary eclipse—a powerful synergy for America, the Moon child (a.k.a., Cancerian). Like all other signs, all Cancerians have a shadow side, yet it's their love and light that make this country great.[83]

---

82 Christopher Brooks, "Chapter 10: The Scientific Revolution," in *Western Civilization: A Concise History*, (2019; Pressbooks, 2020), accessed March 8, 2024, https://pressbooks.nscc.ca/worldhistory/chapter/chapter-10-the-scientific-revolution/.

83 Daniel Louis Duncan, "Planetary Alignment and the Meaning of July 4th," Medium, July 4, 2018, https://rousseauman123.medium.com/https-historicalgenealogy-blogspot-com-2018-07-planetary-alignment-and-meaning-of-july-html-62721d324474.

The New York Stock Exchange was "born" under the sign of Taurus on May 17, 1792.[84] That date might seem insignificant, but the Exchange's symbol is a big bull, and the astrological symbol of Taurus also is a bull. It seems like a little more than a coincidence.

Even the NASA space program was developed because people were looking up and wondering how to get to the stars and the moon. That wonder, that view of the cosmos, led to so many technological and societal advancements on a scale we don't see as commonly anymore. Sadly, many people are more concerned with the release of the next iPhone than whether or not the space program is advancing.

Arguably, looking at the skies and studying the cosmos have led to some of humanity's greatest leaps forward in civilization, innovation, and technology. Even in modern-day endeavors, the cosmos play a role.

POWERFUL MEN USE THE COSMOS FOR IMPORTANT DECISIONS

Maybe that all sounds like ancient history, but we see evidence of the importance of astronomy and the cosmos all around us today. Daily horoscopes are featured in many large and small publications, many people like to get their astrological birth charts, and some people like to choose careers and life partners based on the zodiac signs.

---

84 "The History of NYSE," NYSE, accessed March 8, 2024, https://www.nyse.com/history-of-nyse.

Statistics point to the turn of the 21st century as a time of astrological awakening for many Americans. A 1999 survey by the National Science Foundation found that 12% of Americans read their horoscopes every day. Another 32% said they read horoscopes occasionally.[85] The American Federation of Astrologers estimated in 2015 that 23% of Americans read their horoscopes daily, almost double the 1999 proportion. It also seems that adversity forces people to look to the cosmos for guidance.[86]

A 2009 survey by the Harris Poll found that 26% of Americans believed in astrology. Compare that to a 1993 study published in the *Journal of the Royal Astronomical Society*, which concluded that 55% of university arts students couldn't distinguish astronomy versus astrology (note: Canadian students were the subjects). Meanwhile, 55% of Americans rejected astrology as pseudoscience in 2012, compared to 62% in 2010, according to the National Science Foundation. When all these numbers are viewed in totality, more people are accepting and open to astrology than ever before.

A growing number of men now make important decisions in their lives based on astrology, particularly horoscopes. Seeing who does what based on their astrological sign is an interesting pastime and has some value when I work with clients. For instance, according to astrology, Aries are said to make decisions based on personal values and gut feelings. Those born under the sign of Taurus are more practical and often make the safest choice. Geminis are

---

85   "Newest Survey Shows Most Americans Have Confidence in Science but Lack Understanding," Office of Legislative and Public Affairs, June 19, 2000, https://www.nsf.gov/od/lpa/news/press/00/pr0045.htm.

86   Linda Rodriguiz McRobbie, "How Are Horoscopes Still a Thing?" *Smithsonian Magazine*, January 5, 2016, https://www.smithsonianmag.com/history/how-are-horoscopes-still-thing-180957701/.

indecisive people. They make decisions based on social harmony—meaning choices that make others feel good. But astrology goes far beyond just horoscopes.[87]

Larry Schwimmer is an astrologer and advisor to Fortune 500 C-level executives. He touts himself as a "new voice" that combines business savvy with the metaphysical world to help important people live more complete, fulfilling lives. He wrote frequently about planetary alignments from 2012–2015 that kept pointing to radical revolution, similar to cultural events of the 1960s. Occupy Wallstreet and the Tea Party were both prominent during Schwimmer's time of writing. He also explained how the planets influence the economy, presidential elections, global events, and personal lives.[88]

Many great men had someone like Schwimmer in their lives to interpret the cosmos and apply those conclusions to their lives. Astrology appeals to some very powerful and influential people.

RONALD REAGAN

Two months into his presidency, Ronald Reagan got the scare of his life. It was March 30, 1981. John Hinckley, Jr. was a 25-year-old college dropout who was obsessed with actress Jodi Foster. He thought the best way to get Foster's attention was by assassinating the president. Hinckley shot President Reagan in front of the Washington Hilton Hotel that day. He also shot Press

---

87   "Zodiac Signs and Astrology Signs Meanings and Characteristics," ZodiacSign, accessed March 8, 2024, https://www.zodiacsign.com/.

88   "Larry Schwimmer," Larry Schwimmer, accessed March 8, 2024, https://www.astrodecision.com/.

Secretary James Brady, Secret Service Agent Tim McCarthy, and a police officer. President Reagan was treated and released from the hospital less than two weeks later. But the event changed his presidency forever.

First Lady Nancy Reagan first met astrologer Joan Quigley several years earlier during a taping of the *Merv Griffin Show*. Mrs. Reagan contacted Quigley after the assassination attempt on her husband. Quigley told the First Lady that she could have foreseen the incident had she been clued into the Reagans' lives and everyday affairs. She was brought in as an official White House astrologer in 1981. Former Chief of Staff Donald Regan wrote in his 1988 memoir that "virtually every major decision" by President Reagan was first cleared by Quigley based on her planetary observations.[89]

Quigley brought new attention to astrology as major media covered her for years after her stint in the White House.[90]

RAYMOND MERRIMAN AND J. P. MORGAN

"Millionaires don't need astrologers, but billionaires do." Those are the famous words attributed to banker J. P. Morgan, implying that humanity has no control over economic happenings. It all is controlled by the cosmos. Morgan surrounded himself with

---

89   Donald T. Regan, *For the Record: From Wall Street to Washington* (San Diego: Harcourt Brace Jovanovich, 1988).

90   Jessica Weisberg, "Joan Quigley, Ronald Reagan's Guide to the Stars," *The Paris Review*, June 4, 2018, https://www.theparisreview.org/blog/2018/06/04/joan-quigley-ronald-reagans-guide-to-the-stars/; "Millionaires Don't Need Astrology. Billionaires Do," *The Bean Magazine*, June 5, 2022, https://beanmagazine.org/weekly-spotlight/f/millionaires-dont-need-astrology-billionaires-do.

astrologers to help him make major decisions on investments and business.[91]

Raymond Merriman takes a similar approach. Merriman, president of Merriman Market Analyst (MMA), told *Forbes* in 2012 that his clients covet his analysis, which is largely based on planetary cycles and "geocosmic market turning points." Despite all of his clients being financial market geniuses, they all understand that the cosmos gives them an edge over the competition.[92]

SELF-AWARENESS AND THE COSMOS

Like everyone else these days, I personally spend a lot of time in my head and looking down at my phone and not looking up. And I know that there's going to be different people in this world based off the abundance in their area toward modern-day conveniences. So, people living in a rural area versus Los Angeles have a different pace and a different digital connection. In L.A., they've got billboards on every corner. A lot of them are lit up with bright lights. In more rural areas, there aren't as many lights or external digital stimuli.

Man-made light is distracting, and all those artificial lights reduce what can be seen in the night sky—sometimes completely. In some major cities, it is impossible to see stars at all because of the constant artificial light around the clock. We all got shoved into the digital world, and we didn't actually

91   "J. P. Morgan and Astrology," *Karen Christino* (website), accessed April 26, 2024, https://karenchristino.com/evangeline-adams/j-p-morgan-and-astrology/.

92   Kenneth Rapoza, "Can Planets Affect Your Portfolio?," Forbes, February 20, 2012, https://www.forbes.com/sites/kenrapoza/2012/02/20/can-planets-affect-your-portfolio/?sh=3b17ffc615e1.

consciously choose a strategy to deal with the accompanying changes.

We should be looking up more, not down. I always think about it the same way as with fasting. I like to take it back to the cave days, where darkness was darkness, and there's nothing you're going to do about it. You'll have to get outside to utilize the daylight and hopefully put in a good day's work.

In today's world we don't always have that kind of drastic transition. We turn on the light, we continue to work, and we grind harder. With artificial light, we no longer have to live by the cycles of sun and moon, night and day, and it changes our awareness about what's above us in the skies. So, it's just about being self-aware on that level.

I'm always thinking about how much I'm looking down. As a photographer, I was always looking down through a camera lens or at the digital screen. When I had my neck injury, I was almost forced to look down. Now, I have to be extra aware of not looking down because looking down is part of my job. How many people out there also have that condition as part of their job? How many of them are aware of a need for balance and can make that conscious transition?

Most of the time, when people are looking down, it seems like they are looking at something digital, a phone, a tablet, an e-reader, etc. And now it seems that people in their 20s have neck problems, eyesight issues, and other bodily problems that could be contributed to looking down.[93] I think about the state of peoples' necks today compared to what peoples' necks were like 30, 40, or 50 years ago. I'm just amazed at that process and what it's done to us. The problems are starting in their 20s, and they aren't realizing it's their jobs on top of looking down at their digital devices that are creating the problems.

And if they're not aware, they won't do the self-care on whatever level they need in order to counter the ill effects. It's like throwing your health to the wind. So, when I hear about the first analog computer, I'm like, "Yeah, it makes a ton of sense. We were looking up, fixed on the stars."

NEW YEAR'S DAY: START ENVISIONING ON OCTOBER 1

While my 21-day program always starts on a new moon or a full moon, cosmic cycles aren't limited to the lunar month. They can also be seen in the calendar solar year.

December 31 is traditionally a day of excess indulgence in the Western world. Kids love staying up late, while some adults try their best to make it to midnight after long days of drinking. January 1 marks the New Year, the time for renewal, resetting, and reflection.

The first New Year's Eve celebration is said to have taken place circa 2,000 BCE in Ancient Mesopotamia. It was an 11-day festival

---

93   "Neck Pain or Stiffness," Seattle Children's Hospital, October 11, 2023, https://www.seattlechildrens.org/conditions/a-z/neck-pain-or-stiffness/.

during the March (vernal) equinox, the last half of the month. It makes perfect sense. Spring in the Northern Hemisphere is a time of renewal. Bears wake up from hibernation, flowers are blooming, and animals are mating. Thus, the Mesopotamian New Year coincided with natural phenomena that happened every year.[94]

Many cultures saw September as the time to plan for New Year's for subsequent execution in October and the remainder of the Gregorian year. The idea was that the year ended in October because that's when all the leaves fell off the trees, the last harvests were in, and the world was "dying," preparing to be born again, or renewed, in the springtime.

Thus, October and fall were times to prepare for the upcoming renewal.

Rosh Hashanah is the Jewish New Year. It is always celebrated sometime in September or the first few days of October. Enkutatash is the New Year holiday in Eritrea and Ethiopia. It takes place on September 11 or 12 every year. In an article that Anne Marie Chaker published in the *Wall Street Journal* in 2016, she pointed out how September is back-to-school time. But she also cited studies showing that September is when people join gyms most often and is the month people decide to change careers.[95]

---

94   Jonathan Vankin, "The New Year's Holiday Explained: From Mesopotamia to Temecula, How We Celebrate the New Year," California Local, December 30, 2021, https://californialocal.com/localnews/statewide/ca/article/show/2078-new-year-celebration-calfornia-explained/.
95   Anne Marie Chaker, "September Is the Real New Year," *Wall Street Journal*, September 14, 2016, https://www.wsj.com/articles/september-is-the-real-new-year-1473875636.

I could never figure out why I would want to start any new goal or resolution on January 1.

Recently, I started to rein myself in with my training and I was like, "Come on, man. I know you came off being injured. I know you're scared to get injured again. I get it, but let's go, let's work a little harder." I told myself to hit my IMS training when I hit the showers, hit my affirmation when I'm training, hit my affirmation when I wake up and make it supercharged and reflexive. I did, and I was able to get in a higher frequency and move from alpha to beta. I was able to push harder and then I perked up.

I realized that I hadn't been in high-performance mode. Since my injury, I had been telling myself, "You'll get back there." But I wasn't pushing myself. I was nurturing myself back to good health, and I wasn't so aggressive with my training. As soon as I started to feel like I needed to commit to going harder than what I had been doing, I noticed my thinking really wasn't as clear as it could be. My frequency wasn't as clean as it could be. That's when I was like, "Oh man, this is conscious command. I was a bit more unconscious than I had realized, but I'm getting back into the pocket. Here we go!"

The outcome got me thinking about how if I was just a little bit off like this in the months of November or December because I decided to do some holiday celebrating, breaking from my fasting and exercise routine, by January 1, I wouldn't be where I should be in terms of conscious command. If you start January 1 like that, just coming off of being lax, you're not at conscious command, which is why so many New Year's resolutions run out of steam.

If you get in a lax state just weeks before a big endeavor, it's not high performance. Then you try to start out at high performance straight from being lax. It isn't going to work because you haven't given yourself the time to work back from that lax, celebratory mindset around the holidays. Just like I needed to work back to a high-performance state after being in a nurturing mindset after my injury.

It's not so much the things you do to celebrate that are the problem. Everyone enjoys a good break from their routine around the holidays. Whether it is taking a break from exercising, eating foods they wouldn't normally eat, or drinking a little more than usual, those actions aren't the enemy. It's the moment you say, "I'm going to take a break" that you've lost the momentum. Whether it is conscious or not, necessary or not, that's the moment that changes everything. What happens is the moment you think about taking a break, your body and nervous system follow suit, and you've already checked out of high performance. I had to slow down after my injury, and I didn't even realize how it impacted me until later.

So, if you check out for two weeks around the holidays, especially that week between Christmas and New Year's when a lot of people have paid time off and their work offices are closed, and you got your nervous system lax, you can forget about moving into high performance on January 1. No one can just jump into high performance like the flip of a switch.

The best practice is for "New Year's resolutioners" to begin visualizing and practicing for your New Year's goals as early as possible—preferably at the beginning of October—and work to accommodate the slow-down between the holidays.

THE JANUARY NEW YEAR

The ancient Roman calendar also celebrated the New Year in March, in accordance with the lunar cycle. Sosigenes of Alexandria was an astronomer from Egypt who claimed Greek nationality. Details of his life are scant. What is generally agreed upon by historians is that Sosigenes consulted Julius Caesar in designing the Julian Calendar to follow the solar year instead of the lunar year. The new calendar took effect on January 1 in 709 *anno urbis conditae* (AUC), the equivalent of 45 BCE. There was no astrological or other significance for choosing the date as the New Year. It was simply mandated by Caesar and remains to this day.[96]

A December 2019 survey by YouGov found that a good majority of New Year's resolutions have something to do with losing weight and being healthier overall.[97] Saving money is also a common resolution. January represents winter, cold, and inactivity. It's impractical on its face for January to facilitate renewal and revival. That's why a 2018 survey published by Statista found that only 4% of Americans fulfilled their resolutions.[98]

So, we know almost everyone who began on January 1 fizzles out by March. But if we start in October and fizzle by December, we get an update on January 1 for another burst in motivation. If you want to hop on that "new year, new me" wagon, it's easier when you start the

---

96   "Did You Know?," COPS Office E-Newsletter 7, no. 1 (January 2014), https://cops. usdoj.gov/html/dispatch/01-2014/did-you-know.asp.

97   Jamie Ballard, "Exercising More and Eating Healthier Are This Year's Most Popular New Year's Resolutions," YouGov, December 13, 2018, https://today.yougov.com/ society/articles/22168-new-years-resolutions-2019-exercise-healthy-eating.

98   Martin Armstrong, "The Most Common New Year's Resolutions for 2018," Statista, January 2, 2018, https://www.statista.com/chart/12386/the-most-common-new-years -resolutions-for-2018/.

cycle back in October. It takes the awareness of our calendar system and how it was set up as well as awareness of how we might move within energy and the seasons. Ask yourself, "Are you sluggish during the winter?" Maybe you are, maybe you're not. If you are, then you're not a person who needs to ask yourself on January 1 to get up and start being active. You need to start earlier, like back in October.

I started thinking, "Man, I'm a sluggish person during the winter." That's just me, that's my pattern. Other people have a higher ability to maintain their activity and energy throughout the winter. Some people find themselves more sluggish in the spring or summer. Since I'm most sluggish in the winter, I'm like, "Why would I start a goal during that time period and expect high performance from myself?"

> *Autumn carries more gold in its pocket than all the other seasons.*
>
> — **Jim Bishop**

I don't see a ton of people getting excited about the New Year and New Year goals, or the winter months. I really see people getting excited about the fall and in particular, spooky season. There's a lot of energy. I don't necessarily see that in those January, February months.

Kids are going back to school in September. Its timing looks and feels like a hard transition just prior to another change in season. You would think the same would go for our biggest goal-setting time of year. But at the beginning of January, it doesn't feel like that hard of a transition. In fact, it can feel anticlimactic.

So, I started questioning, what is this January 1 thing? It led me into the research of looking at all these things. From what I could see, the date was selected for religious reasons, power reasons. It wasn't because it was the best way to align your goals and effort with the Earth's seasons and the cosmos, I can tell you that.

Julius Caesar set up his stuff the way he wanted it, not necessarily the way it moves for the people. Here in America, the way we move and the way that energy is, I think it's a lot more beneficial to go back to the way that many of the cultures that I've listed in this chapter celebrated the new-year energy. There's many other different religions that will celebrate the New Year in September or October. They follow the energy flow of the year and the seasons.

Now, I always jump into the January 1 mindset in early October. I like to start putting in the serious work well before I hit Jan 1. When I get after it with that kind of energy, with that frequency, I find I move and finish the calendar year strong. By the time I hit January 1, I can pull back into more of a marathon pace, which to me represents what I see with bears hibernating. Like them, I'm going to chill a little bit. But only because I've consciously created that positive residual window for myself in the months just prior.

Within that positive residual window, I'm going to do the conscious work so that I can keep the forward momentum going. It's the difference between getting success consciously versus unconsciously.

Without momentum, we're doomed. There're many thought leaders online who talk about momentum. As I talked about with false pedestals, you have to obtain momentum consciously or it will get pulled out from under you. January 1 is supposed to be a time to get conscious where I think a lot of people don't get conscious, they just get actionable. Holiday excuses or not, they just practiced being lax. So, of course it's easy to get actionable, unconsciously. And it's easy to find yourself going, "Oh, shit. What happened? I had these January 1 goals…"

How many New Year's resolutions have you made and stuck with? I've seen a lot of gyms and workout programs with an influx of subscribers in January with more than 50% dropping off by March because people only got into it as a New Year resolution.

These types get so busy trying to ramp themselves up and get to the action that they didn't do any conscious or momentum work. I started recognizing it early on in my coaching career. Some of the personal development work I do today is geared toward the end of the year timeframe. It gives clients focus well before the January 1 energy arrives, to come into self, and to come into purpose. That process gets them to know what it's like to ride out the end of the year strong with conscious command.

HOW MANY MOONS?

I was well into my practice of anchoring purpose with the moon when I read that in the average human lifetime, any person only gets about 1,000 full moons.[99] At that point I hadn't questioned or calculated how many times I would be updating my purpose; I

---

99   Trevor Kjorlien, "1000 Full Moons," Plateau Astro, January 17, 2021, https://plateauastro.com/blog/2021-01-17/1000-full-moons.

just knew I liked the rhythm and results. But the 1,000 full moon or "check points realization" helped me to better understand my studies of the moon cycles and the energy behind it.

A lot of people will notice the full moon and celebrate certain full moons, with posts all over social media about the next blue moon, super moon, and all kinds of full-moon-related news. But a lot of people forget there's a new moon in the moon cycle. So, I always make sure to put up those new moon posts for everyone to see and honor.

If you don't know anything about the new moon, it's a good opportunity to pivot and start learning about the new moon. It's the first step forward in the right direction toward being a little bit more aware of something in the pitch-black night. Even if you can't see the new moon, your awareness of it exists, and its effects can be felt like a full moon.

There's more stuff happening in the night sky than you think. That big, shining aspect can become reflexive to your purpose. How many opportunities do we have other than just January 1 to think about a goal and a purpose? How many opportunities or how many symbolizing windows have we set up in our world to trigger purpose?

I have to have triggers. That's why I've turned the full moon and new moon into regular "purpose-driven check-in points" for myself. I don't have to wait around for January 1. I just have to wait for the next moon cycle and treat it with that special Jan 1 commitment and feeling. Seeing the full moon is a visual reminder, but being aware of the new moon should be another conscious reminder. Look for both phases online.

Those 1,000 full moons and 1,000 new moons in an average lifetime mean you also have 2,000 chances to think about your purpose, your direction, and pivot—rather than just the significantly fewer you might have if you only wait for January 1.

With our self-sabotaging tendencies, we should work to make these trigger points reflexive, so that we're constantly thinking about and updating our purpose. The full moon is usually very blatantly clear in the sky but even if it's completely hidden, it can help us get reflexive in our purpose. Ditto for the new moon, which will never been seen when in that phase. Regardless, just as the IMS can be reflexive, so should purpose, but you have to find that process for yourself.

It's all a sliding scale. It's like the zero-to-cocksure scale, only you're sliding within the cosmos. And for those who connect to it or could connect to it, it's a huge anchor. You can catch the full-moon energy and then jump to new-moon energy. New moon for new intentions and new beginnings. The moon cycles are like a ski lift going round and round. Catch and ride them with your purpose.

For me, I couldn't do it without the moon cycles because focusing on January 1 isn't enough. It's one day and in the thick of winter. Three months later, no one is talking about the new year anymore. Then, the focus is all about quarterly taxes, and yearly or quarterly purpose and intentions quickly get overridden by the mundane. Since that one day wasn't enough, I had to look for something else. And as we all need to look for something to become reflexive within our purpose, the moon was a really good choice for me.

CONSCIOUS COMMAND PRE-NEW YEAR AND PURPOSE CHECKPOINTS

Great is the art of beginning, but greater the art is of ending.

— Henry Wadsworth Longfellow, "Elegiac Verse"

The U.S. is not changing its New Year's traditions anytime soon. Still, purposeful men and women can control the way it's utilized and how it impacts their lives. Those who begin planning their New Year in September have 90 days and roughly three full moons and three new moons of momentum by the time January 1 rolls around. While others are just starting out, you'll have been in full sprint mode for over 12 weeks.

Surviving the holidays with conscious command is like, as the saying goes, making it in New York City: "If you can make it here, you can make it anywhere." I say that if you can make it through the holidays with conscious command, you can make it through any other month or holiday season. Conscious command will let you know what days to let loose on during the holidays and when it's time to get yourself in line. It can provide your various holiday seasons with both balance and joy. And if it's favorable, you can let up and move into a marathon pace in January when the energy is lower in frequency. Furthermore, 90 days is plenty of time to form new habits or cease bad ones. You will certainly finish the year strong *and* begin the next one with conscious command.

If you tie the moon cycles into your regular check-ins, you'll be even more aware of your purpose and be able to consciously and reflexively make the most of conscious command. Want to dive in a little deeper? You can further strategize purpose based on the timing and movements of the other celestial bodies. No matter what path you take, try to keep your head up a little bit more… your purpose might be waiting right in front of you.

CHAPTER 9

THE IMS AND FULFILLING LIFE'S PURPOSE

To begin to think with purpose, is to enter the ranks of those strong ones who only recognize failure as one of the pathways to attainment.

— **James Allen**, *As a Man Thinketh*

Herman Melville, the writer of *Moby Dick*, had no idea he'd write such an iconic, classic novel. The irony was that during his lifetime, he never saw the book reach its full potential. Did Herman Melville think his book was a failure?

I don't believe so. When he wrote that final page and got his story out in completion, I'd say he saw it as a success. He kept working at it—he was all in on completing his book. When you dedicate yourself to something that fully, it becomes a life purpose, a life path. I'm certain that Herman Melville saw the completion of his book, and its publication, as a success, regardless of how it performed in sales prior to his death.

More than that accomplishment, he fulfilled a life purpose, which alone breeds success and garners more feelings of accomplishment. But you have to see it through to the end.

Just wanting something badly enough doesn't mean you'll get there if it isn't aligned with your life path. On the flip side, you have to want something badly enough to make it happen. You have to ask yourself, "Is this really my purpose? Is this really what I want to work toward?"

The American Dream is what everyone is striving for, in one way or another. But what does it really translate into? For many, the traditional American Dream it's a house in the suburbs and the "All American" family, complete with working 9–5 Monday to Friday until retirement at age 65. If that's the real American Dream, it's not my dream. And I know plenty of others who don't want or feel drawn to that cookie-cutter lifestyle.

Unfortunately, I also know a lot of people who are adamant that the American Dream is the path to success. But everyone has to define success for themselves. Yet, both defining success and defining the American Dream are as subjective as finding your life's purpose.

Early on I had a teacher at the American Conservatory Theater who said, "Don't confuse your commercial success with your personal success." I took his words to mean that even if I became a superstar actor in my acting days, it had no bearing in my success in my outside relationships, family, personal growth, or anything other than my career. Too many people confuse career success with overall success, but each area of life requires a different level of attention and what success means to you.

Today, I still see a lot of people drawn to the traditional American Dream, especially people from other countries looking to relocate to America. I'm also seeing a big shift within younger generations in America who reject the traditional American Dream and have started forging their own, new American Dream focused more on following passions, not working their life away, and living a more fluid lifestyle. Like success, that American Dream can mean something different to everyone.

WHY DO I TALK ABOUT PURPOSE?

By definition, purpose can be an innate spiritual connection or a cerebral understanding and commitment. Either way, purpose must be curated.

If we were lucky, we made connecting to purpose our very first goal on the path to self-development, and the connection sustained many more goals in its wake. If we weren't so lucky, we only set goals for ourselves and ignored our attention to purpose. When we lack or lose a connection to purpose, we fail to set and accomplish goals over an extended period. The waters get murky, and our success falters.

To make the IMS positively charged and reflexive takes hard work—especially when a story of lack and limitation is dominating our lives. A good connection to purpose, though, can get us committed and moving in the right direction. A strong sense of purpose drives meaning and action even when no clear path or strategy exists. It gets us up off the ground and ready to accomplish the goals we start setting for ourselves.

It's important to remember that goals are short-lived, while with purpose, it can mean a lifetime. Our relationship with purpose should be our absolute best relationship, and getting intimate with our purpose as often as possible helps to keep that spark alive.

Look into your values and beliefs; you might find your purpose.

I'm amused when people tell me that they aren't on a diet, but also stress about their intake of carbs, protein, and inability to avoid chocolate. As if the word "diet" just meant eating salads. Diet is whatever and however much you eat. Essentially, we all are on a diet. The same goes for purpose. We all have one, whether we call it that or not. Ever wonder if you do or do not have a purpose? Well, purposeful people are said to have strong values and beliefs. And that sounds like many of us at one point or another for one reason or another.

If you have strong values and beliefs or admire someone else's values and beliefs and would like to embody them someday, you can find a purpose.

FINDING PURPOSE

Finding purpose makes me think of the word polymath, which means being good at many things. Purpose evolves and changes as you go through personal development. Your purpose could be many different things over the course of your life, just like being a polymath who is good at many different things. Lev Vygotsky, the father of self-talk, was a great example of a polymath. He had made his marks in philosophy, politics, and psychology by the time he passed at the age of 37.

Think of it like this: If I'm experiencing some kind of lack or disruption in my finances or my relationships, I switch my focus to the area that is having trouble. My purpose is altered because what I need to do to balance different areas of my life is going to differ for each area. I start to fine tune the areas that need the most work.

Usually, I can follow astrology and the cosmos to direct my purpose. Other times, I can feel it in my heart or by intuition. I kind of go, "Okay, this needs attention right now. Let me fine tune this area in my life right now." To be clear, let's take the description that is placed at the end of the IMS affirmation in chapter 4.

"(Fill in Full Name)______________ is an accomplished, successful, well-respected, continuously sought-after, thriving, expansive (Fill in Desired Affirmative Statement) _____________________."

I might have a "big-purpose" word that I place at the end, like a word that I am always coming back to. But sometimes, I'll bring in a new word that drives my focus toward whatever needs my immediate attention. I use that new word at the end of my affirmation to make a shift, and sometimes I just look at that word as my only purpose for the moment. I still believe I've got a big, ultimate purpose. But within that affirmation, I also think about, "What's my goal this week or this month?"

I've known so many artists, friends, and clients who sell themselves short. They tell themselves they shouldn't do something because it doesn't feed what they think their purpose is, like how I gave up boudoir and erotic photography. These artists, friends, and clients practice thinking and feeling this way 'til it's reflexive. And I can see that they believe their limitations. It's embedded in their nervous system, and it shows. Over and over my mother said, "God, made me a worrier." She gave up her power to change that, and believe me, it showed.

You have to be all in. You have to be the athlete that this whole book has been talking about. You have to do those special things like working out until 3 a.m. if you have big fitness goals. You have to be intense. But then you have to also know that if you're going to have your hands in many things, it's okay to be that intense. I like to say, "It's a jack-of-all-trades, master of all that we focus in on." And that focus must be intense. You must be obsessive to be a polymath.

What we focus on is based on our IMS moving with the cosmos, dialing into purpose. I couldn't let go of the artist in me, and back when I was looking at self-development coaches like Tony Robbins and comparing myself to them, I tried really hard to let it go. I kept asking myself, "Why am I doing this (nude photography)? When are you going to let it go?" It took me a long time to realize how special it was to be drawn to this kind of photography, and I had to go back to being that guy. Photography, as it turned out, was aligned with my purpose, which is why I couldn't let it go.

At the end of the day, I think that my purpose is to show complexities and to own complexities, and to do both is okay. If you're honoring yourself, then you're going to be living your truth. When you find and accept your purpose, it ties into conscious awareness. You'll start eating better, being happier, and stop feeling like you're swimming against the current. Then, conscious awareness rises because you're on a healthier, clearer path of fulfillment.

Sometimes, without any clear understanding, I think to myself, "For some reason I have to go this way. I have to do this or that. I just know it." And that focus becomes my purpose or a part of it. Is it my purpose to be a father? Yes. Is it my first purpose? Absolutely not. And I've told my family that it's not. I'm very clear, very transparent. My purpose is my work. My purpose is evolution of conscious awareness and bringing people to practice it…to be able to lift everybody else up. That is my purpose. I feel it. And sometimes I might look scattered, like I'm over here doing crazy photo shoots, then I'm over there doing mindset and fitness contests. People could think, "That guy doesn't have a purpose. He's all over the place." But they'd be wrong. Purpose is complex and individual.

THE POWER IN INDIVIDUAL PURPOSE

I watched *Moneyball,* the movie about Billy Beane, the Oakland A's baseball general manager, and it raised some serious questions and thoughts for me at the time. In the movie, his unorthodox approach to building a winning team caught the attention of the Boston Red Sox owner. He gave Beane the opportunity to show the world that his strategies were legit. But in the end, Beane chose not to go to Boston, and the movie portrayed it as choosing to stay in Oakland to be a father for his daughter. It was a move straight out of a pop-culture alpha-male handbook. The Red Sox moved on but used Beane's approach to win the championship shortly there thereafter.[100] Beane chose to be a father, but was it his ultimate purpose? Maybe it was his purpose to give up his sports dreams to be a father—it's hard to say. We all do many things in this life. But it's not like each of us has the same purpose or path.

If your purpose is to have a kid, that's for you to decide. If you have kids but you have a purpose on top of that, you might need to figure out how you can fulfill that purpose *and* be a parent. Many people think that once they have kids, they are the only purpose. I don't believe that. Just as I believe that not everyone that comes into this lifetime is meant to find a soulmate or actually have or want a partner. To me, a soul's purpose is much more complex than just parenthood, family, or relationship status. It goes beyond career choice, geographical location, and day-to-day hobbies.

There was a time when I was pulled away from my daughter Lucy because I felt that my purpose was to get to Texas. And at that point, that was the move I had to make. When I had to make that

---

100 "Beane: 'I Never Regretted' Spurning Red Sox, Staying with the A's," NBC Sports, last modified April 8, 2017, https://www.nbcsportsbayarea.com/mlb/beane-i-never-regretted-spurning-red-sox-staying-with-as/1274323/.

decision, I knew that my purpose was everything to me. That's how I operate in this world. The purpose to move to Texas came to me by some sort of greater message, but I had to put myself in that frequency in order to hear it correctly through conscious awareness. Otherwise, such ideas will fuck me up—and have fucked me up many times when I wasn't listening consciously.

At the time, I understood that if I want to get rid of the chaos in my life, I had to act toward a bigger purpose. And so, when that bigger purpose pulled me away from my daughter, it crushed me. But I thought about Billy Beane, and I thought, "Well, shit, if leaving for Texas is part of my purpose and I stay here in California because of my daughter, I would have done what Billy Beane did. He chased a championship his whole life in Oakland after turning down the highest-paid general manager position in Boston, while the Boston team went on to win that championship without him because of his other purpose: his daughter." Which was his bigger purpose?

It felt like my purpose required me to move, and it was a very hard decision to make. When the time came, I didn't take the same choice away from my daughter. One of her good friends had moved to Austin, so her mother and I talked about what Lucy wanted to do. Did she also want to move to Texas or stay in California?

I wanted her to make her own decision, follow her own purpose. At her heart, Lucy is a California girl. She wanted to stay in California. Staying was what her intuition and feelings told her to do, but there was an open discussion with multiple options presented.

I made the move, and I consciously let go of stories of limitation that would otherwise weigh me down. I stepped off that false pedestal of perfect parenthood and stepped into the alpha mindset, following the alpha frequencies, to my greater purpose. I didn't want to "Billy Beane it." I wanted to go for it. That realization didn't make it any easier to move away, but it helped me to continue on my path and confidently live in my purpose.

The most important thing for me was to make sure my daughter knew that I was still there for her. So, with help from her mother, every six weeks, I was on a plane going back and forth between Texas and L.A. so that I could see my daughter. I was still living in a car, by choice this time, and not having to pay rent while working on my own career afforded me the flexibility and means to travel so frequently. Sometimes, only two weeks would go by before I was flying there and back again. Living in a vehicle enabled me to work in another state and still be there whenever I could for my daughter. I was able to pursue my path and live up to my standards as a parent.

The situation makes me think of Earl Nightingale, the self-development radio speaker in the 1950s who said the greatest rewards, whatever those rewards may be, go to the people who take risks. The people getting ordinary jobs and going through a 9–5 process sometimes believe they are reaping the greatest rewards[101]—the American Dream—but they're not. They are just playing it safe.

---

101 "Earl Nightingale | Take Risks Is the Most Intelligent Course to Follow," Dustin Grant YouTube Channel, August 5, 2023, video, 18:40, https://www.youtube.com/watch?v=gYfYcH1qXyU.

It's the risk-takers, the ones who go for something bigger who get the rewards and opportunities, who find the most fulfilling paths. For me to follow my purpose, I had to risk a bad relationship with my daughter. On the other hand, if I didn't take that risk, I never would have established my programs and I may have never completed this book—two purposes.

Sometimes, clients I work with will ask me, "What if I don't know my purpose?" I know that to keep moving forward and trying to figure it out is not easy. In response to their question, I ask "What do you care about?" Purpose doesn't have to come from the grand, innate feeling like how I knew I had to move to Texas.

Jordan Peterson, the Canadian psychologist and author, isn't someone I naturally gravitate to and follow, but I do know that he is held in high regard by a lot of people. And I know that Peterson talks a lot about how we'd all be better off if we had something to care and get excited about.[102] For me, his words ring true. The point is that you've got to keep moving until you do find something you care about. Maybe you're not going to find and hook that big purpose. Maybe it is a smaller-scale purpose based off the idea that just having one is a good thing. Any purpose is going to organize you a little bit more…you're going to have less chaos in your life.

> *If you can tune into your purpose and really align with it, setting goals so that your vision is an expression of that purpose, then life flows much more easily.*
>
> — Jack Canfield

---

102 Jordan B. Peterson, *12 Rules of Life: An Antidote to Chaos* (Toronto: Random House Canada, 2018).

I relate it back to sharks. Not all sharks keep moving while they sleep, but the idea is that you're the shark that does. We must always be moving toward our purpose. Sometimes, the movement might look more like drifting than swimming, but you can always dial into your IMS via the celestial bodies for more direction and momentum.

I see the act of staying the course a lot with people making "comebacks." I was reading an old circa 1990 article about the actor John Travolta and how people would see his movies from the '70s and '80s, and think he was still as big a star as ever in the late '80s and early '90s. But in Hollywood around that time, his name was no longer synonymous with the leading man. In interviews, Travolta remained confident in his abilities and direction. So much so that he came off as aloof to his drop in star power. He stayed the course 'til his comeback came around for him.[103]

Surges forward and lulls in between go back to the seasons and cycles. What I realized is that when you stay the course, you can have long gaps, long lows, and what looks like just no fucking success. But you have to be able to sustain your purpose and enthusiasm for years. Because the universe doesn't care about the three- to five-year plan or however long people say it takes to succeed. Your universal timeline might be a little longer, and you're going to need to be able to endure.

I found it interesting that comebacks aren't really comebacks. They're people who wait for the season to change. Let's say the

---

103 Simon Brew, "John Travolta and His Assorted Career Comebacks," Den of Geek, August 4, 2015, https://www.denofgeek.com/movies/john-travolta-and-his-assorted-career-comebacks/.

market is down and so is your portfolio. If you wait for the timing to change, your money will be back up. It's just about being steadfast and being able to get into that goal or purpose kind of mindset that allows you to do what sometimes looks ridiculous. Like me when I was living in a vehicle for five years. I kinda wondered, "How is this going to end? When do I stop this? When do I say I'm not doing this anymore?" Because it got to a point where it became too easy not to do it. I was thriving. I was living in a way that nobody around me was, and through endurance, I was able to do things that people were wishing they were doing.

YOU DON'T HAVE TO CLIMB EVEREST

I want to give people the mindset initiative, but the rest is up to them. I'm just reminding them of who they are and what they are capable of when they acquire the right kind of intention and focus. I want to help people find their purpose by getting them to remember who they are. And we are what we tell ourselves we are. The IMS does that. You want to tell yourself who you are and then start compounding those tiny little wins or "accomplishments." You want to get intimate with the words accomplished and successful. Tell yourself that you are those things and understand how it helps to move you forward. Don't let a big purpose or big ideas outstrip your respect for process and repetition. Part of my purpose is to help clients understand those factors but really to let people get there on their own.

More men fail through lack of purpose than lack of talent.

— **Attributed to Billy Sunday**

There's a concept called "deathbed regrets." It is the five greatest regrets that people have when they find themselves at the end of their lives. One of the top five regrets is wishing they did more with their lives. I relate that perspective directly back to purpose. If you don't take risks, take opportunities, and follow your purpose, you get stuck and end up wishing you did more with your life.

To elaborate even more, it's about not getting stuck in one place. Some people think they find their purpose and then cling to it at all costs. But they fail to see their purpose evolving, and they don't grow or change with it, leaving them with feelings of not having done more with their lives. It is the same story I had to break out of when I first gave up boudoir and erotic photography. I tried to push it away over and over again, but I'm glad I went back to it because I don't want to look back on my life and regret cutting out something so important to my purpose.

Test your mettle, test your story.
— **ALPHA PRO by Prodigy Mindset**

To avoid getting stuck and having regrets, you need to be testing your mettle. You need to be testing your internal stories of lack and limitation. I say, "It doesn't have to be climbing Everest." But it can be the same experience in the sense that, say you're doing a plank, and you're trying to get to the point where you're doing them to failure and you're doing them longer than the average time. Let's say the average is three minutes, and you're taking it to six. If you're pushing it like that, then you're experiencing what people experience when they summit Everest but in a shorter amount of time.

In that moment, you hit an extreme, and you didn't have to climb Everest, you didn't have to do the Ironman. The same is true of your purpose. It doesn't have to be as big as climbing Everest, but to achieve it, you still have to do the training, the work, and adapt to different circumstances in order to get there. You also have to test yourself and your stories, take risks. You can test a story by just saying you're going to put in 10 minutes more than what the average person is putting in, whether it's a workout, and exercise, studying a language, etc.

Get out of the idea that it has to be for so long, and it has to be so grand like summitting Everest. Some ambitions are too big for people. So, you need to step it back. But you also need to make it intense. If you have a story that you really need to rewrite and you are having a hard time making things reflexive, it's about going all the way down into that abyss, it's about those long, one-set-to-failure sessions, and really working on rewriting that story of wanting to quit.

That one rewritten reflexive story alone will elevate you in all other areas of your life. The story of mental limitations can be surpassed just by seeing them and pushing past what you think you know your body and mind can do. That practice alone is going to do so much for so many other stories in your life. It's what really advanced me and got me going.

CHAPTER 10

THE IMS AND TESTING YOUR METTLE

As a mindset coach, I was always talking about injuries that sometimes looked like career-ending injuries and the need to go to work on conscious command in order to give yourself the best opportunity to be that person who can come back at the end of the season and win the gold. Then I got hurt. And I was dealing with the same elements I was talking to my clients about. I was like, "Did I do that to myself? Did I talk and think about it so much that I manifested it? Or was it something I unconsciously knew was coming my way and was preparing for? Was it a direct download from the universe, guiding me in a direction of what I needed to overcome and how I needed to push myself?"

I studied the patterns of events like them enough to conclude that "free will" is the exercise of *attitude* over all events whether they are in our control or not. Curating free will as a process for choosing a good attitude over a bad one in any given circumstance is a far better focus for someone like me. There's certainly no harm in being optimistic about our control over events, but choosing and making a good attitude reflexive under any circumstance is what provides us with real leverage over the unforeseen events in life. That understanding brought me to mettle.

---

met·tle

a person's ability to cope well with difficulties or to face a demanding situation in a spirited and resilient way.[104]

There was a time when I was hiking a lot, but when I got to the top of the mountains, I would have these panic attacks where I couldn't breathe, and I was triggered. In those higher altitudes, I was sent right back to a time when I was younger and someone thought it was funny to suffocate me. At first, I didn't make the connection and I kept trying to climb mountains. I had just finished a lot of the teaching points for our alpha program when I attempted to ascend Mt. Shasta, and I had to go through the IMS process. I had to put it all to work in reflexive manner. I probably looked like a crazy man who lost it on the mountain, but I was going to work on a process I had just developed.

It's always just in the nick of time that I'm developing self-development practices that helped me in these situations.

---

104 Oxford Languages, s.v. "mettle," accessed April 1, 2024, https://www.google.com/search?q=mettle+definition.

Big hikes were something I was into for years while living near the Southern California mountains. With most of my time spent in the city of Los Angeles, I tried to get out often and go on long hikes. I would get lost sometimes, lost to the point where it could've gone bad for me. Luckily, I always found my way back and didn't end up on the news. But I eventually grew to want a bigger challenge with terrain and elevation. A friend of mine was getting into big hikes as well, so we teamed up.

We went for elevation when we picked Mount Elbert in the Colorado Rockies. Some websites list Elbert at 14,439 while others list it at 14,440. I first saw it listed with the three consecutive 4s, and too me, that was divine guidance. We left early, well before sunrise, and we returned just after sunset. The experience was fantastic, but we were looking for something a bit more challenging. Despite being a bit lower in elevation, Mount Shasta came into our conversation, and it spoke to me when I looked it up. I came to find that I had been there before on a fishing trip with my brother. I went to see him after my first attempt on the summit, and he reminded me that Mt. Shasta is where he took me 20 years earlier. And here I was, back again...and then again. I took two attempts on that mountain. The first one was getting altitude sickness, and the second one involved stuff going badly at base camp. It wasn't anything that did me any harm, but it was enough to scare the shit out of me.

The guide service put me in a three-person tent with a married couple. We were setting up the tents at basecamp and the man with whom I would be sharing a tent says, "I fall asleep really quick." He was referring to the fact that we would have to get to bed early and wake up in the middle of the night to start out on our ascent.

I was like, "Oh, wow, okay, cool. Yeah, man, that's great," thumbs up. He gets in there, and sure as shit this guy falls asleep right away. I was like, "Wow." And then he went right into about six variations of snoring in about five-minute intervals. At one point it sounded like he was dying. Then it sounded like he was laughing. I just kept asking myself, "Is this really happening?" On top of that, the gentleman didn't have the most fragrant scent. In a small tent, it was very noticeable, and it gradually grew in presence.

I was stuck in there and I'm thinking, "Okay, I'll be able to Zen out and get myself through this…I can do this." It was working and I was holding my frustration at bay. But after maybe two or three hours in, it was hard to hang on and I realized I just wasn't going to get any sleep.

I was wondering how I was supposed to reach the top of the mountain after staying up all night in frustration. I already had one failed attempt on Mt. Shasta, and that failure was beginning to compound itself in my thinking. I'm going through all this, and eventually I start losing it a little bit. I couldn't breathe and I had to get things off me, my sleeping bag, everything. Then I'm like, I have to get the fuck out of the tent. I go to throw on my boots, and they are a little frozen from standing straight up on the snow.

I was walking around in these two already frozen boots and losing it. I was like, "What are you going to do right now, go down the mountain? You're not going to do that. You need to get to work!"

I knew had to get into the IMS process. I had just completed the design of the ALPHA program, and I was talking to myself about it as I'm losing it. I was so conscious and so unconscious at the same time. It was the most fascinating experience I had ever had with trauma, and it was probably the most needed experience I had in understanding reflexivity, the IMS, and the alpha brain wave. I was using all of it as a firewall.

> *IMS training is an accelerator for those who are ready to make advances and a firewall for those facing adversity. Know your position and know it on a day-to-day basis.*
>
> — **ALPHA PRO by Prodigy Mindset**

By testing my mettle on those big mountain hikes, I was building myself a firewall to combat adversity. And my IMS showed up as a firewall when I couldn't breathe that night at base camp. And at that point trauma flooded into my head that had to do with not being able to breathe. Memories opened up so fast, everything was happening so fast. A flood of suppressed memories came rushing back in, and I felt it all at the same time. And it was at that point that I consciously understood what I needed to do: I better get to work with my IMS. I did, and I ended up finding a sense of calm out there in the snow. And then came this overwhelming feeling of satisfaction from the whole process.

Unfortunately, this one event on the mountain triggered trauma that would go on for years. The experience opened a door inside me where out of nowhere, usually around 2 or 3 a.m., I'm having to get out of the house and into the middle of the street because I can't breathe. But with conscious command, I use the IMS process over and over again to pull me out of my tailspin.

That recovery made me realize that I had to practice the IMS process in between the times when I felt like I was suffocating. I had to prepare and build myself up by testing my mettle. By trying to control the way I counter trauma, I was intentionally setting it off. I would put myself in the state of being triggered. The payoff for that, and testing mettle, is that you get to see your story of trauma loud and clear under absolute fatigue. You get to see it, trap it, and fuel past it with the IMS.

When I say, "Test my mettle," what I'm talking about is one set to failure.

One set to failure provides greater time under tension, and more time under tension triggers an internal story of lack and limitation. Most of the time, you just want to quit because it burns. Actively provoking, and then consciously viewing and shutting down your story of wanting to quit because it burns, can bring up a lot of emotions and triggers. It'll show you if your IMS is reflexive in having your back. For me, I would start panicking while taking a bear crawl to failure. Within 20 minutes I would start thinking, "Am I going to get up and be absolutely manic, just flailing around because I can't breathe?"

I was pushing myself to that point where I had to have that conversation with myself because of past trauma. I had to learn to trap it and move past my fear. And the experience was beautiful. It was a perfect storm of self-development, of seeing and provoking my internal story of limitation. Of how much I could take physically, regardless of my fear of trauma. Being able to shatter one story of limitation by testing yourself will help with every other limiting story you tell yourself, which is why I see the lifestyle of testing your mettle as a type of firewall for future adversity.

The process gets in your nervous system. You're bringing your nervous system into intense mettle training, one-set-to-failure training to provoke the story. And your nervous system is registering that you are shutting down a story. The mental and physical strength that came from that process was second to none. And that's when I just fell in love with testing my mettle. It became a practical tool for keeping internal stories at bay and making the IMS reflexive. I found that I started to get outwardly vocal when pushing myself past my physical limits. The process of testing one's mettle has helped many of the athletes who trained with me to surpass their mental and physical limits. I had no idea that outcome was going to happen. The process was a spiritual one in the sense that these self-development tools were what I needed for my own trauma.

There's still a very small percentage of people who actually summit big mountains like Everest. Most people don't need to climb the mountain to get the same experience those mountains give. People can do it on the ground. It takes conscious work and you have to have a sense of wonder and creativity, of pivoting into new creativity and ideas as I did in testing my mettle with bear crawls. I got into bear crawls out of nowhere. And I was like, "Wow, it's hitting every single muscle. I'm testing my mettle within every single muscle much like a swimmer."

I found in a bear crawl the mental fortitude that comes from that process of not stopping on a big mountain. It was through wonder and creativity that got me to think, "How can I condense that same feeling and effect from a big mountain hike?" The answer came from not putting myself in danger at a high altitude, because I personally have too much trauma that relates to breathing. I don't have that danger if I'm at low altitude in a bear crawl. And I'm still able to reach that same level of testing my mettle.

TESTING YOUR METTLE

Early on, when meditation was my "end all, be all," I viewed big hikes as long walking meditations. I was able to find deeper meaning and connection when the IMS came into light.

When I finally comprehended the immense amount of repetition that someone might need to make their IMS reflexive, I knew one-set-to-failure training was the vehicle. My big hikes were just one long set to failure, and I knew that combining positively charged words with one set to failure, through something like a bear crawl instead of going up a mountain, is going to do more for your nervous system, your trauma, your story, than counting sets, or reps on a bench, or curling while counting to 12.

I'm thinking, "Why would I ever want to spend my time training where I'm only counting sets and numbers?" They don't do anything for me. I definitely feel a spirituality about numbers in my life and in general as well as about the spiritual meaning of numbers, but I don't have a personal connection with counting them out in order while training. It does nothing for my nervous system. I'd rather go deeper than the frequency of numbers. I'd rather focus on my connection to my internal monologue and kill two birds with one stone. In that way, I'm going to take care of a lot of things all at once by fueling my IMS deep into one set to failure.

Testing my mettle became more than physicality. It was testing my ability to pivot into staying positive and to become reflexive.

By testing my mettle, I achieved a level of athleticism that I didn't have in my 20s. Could I have had this achievement in my 20s? Yes, had I been in conscious command and utilizing one set to failure with the IMS.

I've since realized I was never at my full potential. I think I knew it at the time but didn't know what to do about it. And that understanding is partly what drives me today. I knew I didn't live up to my potential in certain areas. But the IMS has allowed me to live up to it now. Let's just say that my recent neck injury does, indeed, limit me from here on out. I am going to look back and be like, "Damn, you were crushing it, brother. And you did it twenty-five years after you were a competitive athlete."

Even if I'm working my ass off the rest of my life to get back to that point before my injury, I'm just happy to have that benchmark to aim for. I set that mark for myself, and it's mine to beat.

I think it is also important to test your mettle on a small level as often as possible. For example, sometimes I'll just do a nine-minute workout. We have nine-minute music tracks at Prodigy Mindset. The idea behind the timing of the track is that nine means completion, spiritually. It's not a true one-set-to-failure workout, but nine minutes is a sufficient amount of time for testing your mettle with one single bodyweight or lightweight movement. That nine-minute mark is a great amount of time to check in and see where your story is at.

TIME UNDER TENSION

When you go to train in a gym, maybe with a personal trainer or on your own, the most common practice is to perform sets and reps of different exercises. You might do three or four sets of 10 squats each or six sets of 15 arm curls.

When I talk about one set to failure, there is no designated set number or repetition number because it is about your personal tolerance levels for overcoming adversity. It is primal, subconscious, and conscious. Yes, there is a physical component, but there's also a spiritual element. You're working within the nervous system, the IMS, your soul, and it's going to elevate you, so it doesn't matter where your focus is. The process helps your focus.

One set to failure should be used beyond the scope of physical endurance and training. I combine concepts like one set to failure with more time under tension when working to exorcise my stories. In the gym, more time under tension refers to a longer duration of time spent exerting yourself.

In conscious awareness, more time under tension is about spending more time with your story, examining it, and consciously breaching limitations. That singular focus right there overrides your nervous system and overrides trauma.

It gets you reflexive toward countering trauma or pivoting from trauma. So, maybe the trauma is never gone. But the ability to want to pivot and to find your strength comes from testing your mettle. The one-set-to-failure and time-under-tension process curates that.

A good number of fitness influencers will do one set to failure, but they're emphasizing muscle growth. What we're talking about is story trapping and making your IMS reflexive. But it has to be conscious. You have to consciously step into that process for that nuanced reason. And if you do, the benefits are profound.

By testing your mettle regularly, you're setting yourself up to win. Adversity is going to be around the corner. It's going to happen, and you can hardly ever predict it. I had no idea that climbing a mountain would trigger me, but it happened. You want to be the person who is always ready to move through the seasons, which are always changing.

Testing your mettle sets you up for being able to endure, to stay on your purpose. If you tap into your alpha brain wave and it's asking you to do something that doesn't look alpha, that's adversity within itself. You're going to have to have some sort of IMS in place to help push you through.

CONCLUSION

When I started getting into film and TV acting, I saw myself as an upcoming action star like Jason Statham, Mark Wahlberg, Vin Diesel, or someone like that. I started spending time on sets becoming other people and characters, taking direction, and being anyone other than myself.

But I realized that I didn't want to keep turning into another character. It was hard enough trying to become myself.

I saw an old Marlon Brando and Dick Cavett interview about the profession of acting. Brando said that acting is a "survival mechanism" and "a daily procedure" for everyone. We all lie, and that is acting. If so, actors are incredible liars. Whether it's on set or on screen, actors don't always show their authentic selves. They take direction on how to stand, what to wear, what to say. On the screen, they play a character that often overshadows who they are as a person.[105]

105   Jonathan Heaf, "Everything You Thought You Knew About Marlon Brando Is a Lie," *GQ*, April 3, 2020, https://www.gq-magazine.co.uk/culture/article/marlon-brando-biography.

Brando took it one step further than that to say we're all acting—we're all trying to save face. We're all trying to just get through the day, and there isn't a single human being who isn't an actor. Everybody is acting, and without that awareness, or empowerment from perspective, it can be very sloppy.[106] I feel like there's some escapism in it. And then there's some empowerment in it as well. We can put in the work to develop ourselves the way an actor would for a role. Overcoming trauma requires that level of commitment and so does reaching great heights—the work looks the same.

I would much rather be Arlen J, because he's better than any character that I would have played on TV. I built my own persona through repetition, telling myself who Arlen J was and is, and thinking and acting with intention and purpose. Coming into my purpose and creating that powerful third-person persona for myself wasn't just a possibility, it's a duty. The same goes for discovering the alpha mindset.

Curating ourselves in that alpha mindset is a duty because we all are one at the end of the day—we're all connected. Based on science, everything is connected. Streamline it all under a microscope…nothing is separated. There's just energy moving with energy. If you curate yourself to become the best you can be with a reflexive IMS and alpha mindset, you're going to end up doing your part for everybody else. That contribution is sometimes the best we can do for others.

---

106   Marlon Brando, interview with Dick Cavett, *The Dick Cavett Show*, June 12, 1973, video, 58:29, https://youtu.be/uU-4wmwc2Rw?si=s9zNSHGVwcuNAX4j.

It's time to write your own story and become your own character through conscious command and the alpha mindset. If you're someone who hasn't thought much of themselves, then you're going to need to get that zero-to-cocksure scale sloped up toward being cocksure. A positively reflexive IMS will do it for you. If you find yourself with your head in the clouds and speaking out of turn, you're going to need to slope yourself down toward zero. Get realistic about where you are and then get to work on your third-person mindset the way an actor would.

In his career, Earl Nightingale talked about how we must be unique individuals and must have individual thoughts. But most of us aren't thinking as individuals because thinking is difficult. Thinking takes creativity, and too many of us avoid our creativity because it is based in our lack of conscious command. Finding a strong purpose, keeping your focus on it takes a lot of thought and a lot of telling yourself, "My thoughts are worth it, not just for me but for everyone else."[107] The conclusion I got from Earl Nightingale was don't conform to the thinking of the masses, purpose takes risk, and you will find purpose as you become the individual you were meant to be. When you do that, you become your own character, like I became Arlen J. Like Earvin Johnson, the more "Magic" came to life, it was easier for him to exist as that person, and it was easy for people to believe he was that person. And I really see no difference with Arlen J. It takes real work, but it's worth every second in the end.

---

107 Earl Nightingale, "There Is Only One You | Earl Nightingale," Sherman Rivers YouTube Channel, January 10, 2023, video, 7:24, https://www.youtube.com/watch?v=Y3oCcNvD0LA.

Everyone's journey is going to look different, but reaching your goals, finding your boundaries and personal development, goes beyond helping yourself. In a world where we all are connected, personal development helps everyone. The correct and accurate definition of an alpha is a highly conscious being who is a beneficial presence to themselves and society. That alpha is the dark horse in the race for the enlightenment of mankind.

But the work never stops. You have to start every day with the conscious awareness and intention to keep working in order to become your own character with purpose and conscious command.

Zero-Zero.

ACKNOWLEDGMENTS

In my first year of college, a friend asked me what I wanted to do with my life. I said, "I want to be a non-fiction writer."

Life's complexities have always fascinated me, yet for many years, I floundered and experienced long bouts of writer's block. I eventually understood that my lack of self-awareness, a.k.a. conscious command, stifled my confidence and creativity.

Maya Angelou once said, "You can't use up creativity. The more you use, the more you have." This quote resonates deeply with me as I reflect on my journey.

I want to thank those who pierced the veil and gave me the foresight and assurance that I would one day get here.

Together, let's master your
MINDSET

 Join Arlen's mailing list to get more insights, tips and resources on mastering conscious command and developing an alpha mindset at **arlenj.com**.

 Start your training in Conscious Command with a 21-day mindset initiative program at **prodigymindset.com**

 Order discounted bulk purchases of this book for your company, organization, or community at **arlenj.com**.

 Book Arlen for speaking events at **arlenj.com**.

CONNECT WITH ARLEN AT

Instagram: @prodigymindsetgym

Instagram: @arlenjmindset

Facebook: Arlen J

Youtube: Arlen J

THANK YOU FOR READING!

If you enjoyed *The Inner Path to Alpha*, please leave a review on Goodreads or on the retailer site where you purchased this book.